Praise Quotes

Becoming Quantum Safe is a timely and enlightening book that brings quantum readiness into sharp business focus. It turns uncertainty into clarity with a practical roadmap for discovering cryptographic risks, transitioning securely, and maintaining trust. Executives will find this book empowering and essential in navigating the seismic shifts that come with quantum computing.

—Rob Thomas, SVP Software and
Chief Commercial Officer, IBM

Quantum computing is rewriting the rules of cybersecurity. *Becoming Quantum Safe* breaks down the complexity of post-quantum cryptography and offers a strategic plan any business leader can follow. With real-world guidance and regulatory foresight, it's a powerful tool to lead confidently and stay ahead of emerging cryptographic threats.

—Jamie Thomas, Chief Client Innovation Officer,
Enterprise Security Executive, IBM

Becoming Quantum Safe isn't just about preparing for tomorrow—it's about protecting your business today. It empowers leaders to understand the advancement and advantage of quantum computing, drive crypto-modernization, and align with global regulatory demands. It's a rare blend of strategic insight and technical depth that belongs in every executive's digital transformation toolkit.

—Jay Gambetta, IBM Fellow and
VP of Quantum

This book is precisely what every technical leader needs to understand and address the quantum threat. *Becoming Quantum Safe* cuts through the complexity, offering practical, step-by-step strategies to ensure your business remains secure and compliant. The quantum threat is no longer theoretical. This practical guide is essential reading for anyone serious about future-proofing their cryptographic infrastructure.

—Ravi Srinivasan, CEO – Votiro, Investor, and Advisor in Cybersecurity

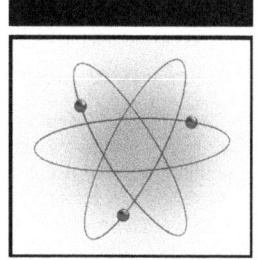

Becoming Quantum Safe

Protect Your Business and Mitigate Risks with Post-Quantum Cryptography and Crypto-Agility

Jai Singh Arun
Ray Harishankar
Walid Rjaibi

Foreword by Whitfield Diffie,
co-inventor of public key cryptography

WILEY

Published by John Wiley & Sons, Inc., Hoboken, New Jersey.
Published simultaneously in Canada and the United Kingdom.

ISBNs: 9781394374328 (hardback), 9781394374342 (ePDF), 9781394374335 (ePub)

For general information on our other products and services or for technical support, please contact our Customer Care Department within the United States at (800) 762-2974, outside the United States at (317) 572-3993 or fax (317) 572-4002. For product technical support, you can find answers to frequently asked questions or reach us via live chat at https://support.wiley.com.

If you believe you've found a mistake in this book, please bring it to our attention by emailing our Reader Support team at wileysupport@wiley.com with the subject line "Possible Book Errata Submission."

Wiley also publishes its books in a variety of electronic formats. Some content that appears in print may not be available in electronic formats. For more information about Wiley products, visit our web site at www.wiley.com.

Library of Congress Control Number: 2025942812

Cover image: © Boris25/Getty Images
Author photos: Courtesy of the Authors
Cover design: Wiley

Jai Singh Arun

To Mrs. Saroopi Devi, my mother—whose love was our universe, raising eight lives with quiet power and infinite grace.

To my father, Mr. Phusiya Ram —whose hands built dreams from dust, giving everything so we could reach the stars.

To Varshal, my heart's constant—life partner for over 25 years, and the silent architect of our family's joy and love. You carried the weight so I could carry words.

To Saachi, our radiant daughter, shaping the future through science, music and soul.

To Yogya, our curious son—driven by tech and business, and the rhythm of the soccer game.

To my brothers Ramesh, Vijay, and the late Mr. Om Prakash, and my sisters Sunita, Anita, Vinita, and the late Ms. Babita—your affection is my compass.

And to Mrs. Chitra Mayekar, Suchita, Amey, and the late Mr. Chandrahas Mayekar—thank you for the endearment and boundless support.

You are all the soul behind these pages.

Ray Harishankar

*To my mom and dad Saraswathi and Raman, who have always been my
inspiration and exemplified the meaning of "defiant in defeat but
magnanimous when victorious".*

*To my wife Prema for her understanding and unwavering support
over the years.*

*To my daughters Krupa and Keerthi who brighten my every day
with their love.*

Walid Rjaibi

*To my late father, who gently guided me toward mathematics and
cryptography, planting the seeds of a lifelong passion.*

*To my mother, whose unwavering love and wisdom have been a constant
source of strength.*

*To my wife, whose patience, encouragement, and belief in me have
sustained this journey.*

*To my children, Saif, Safa, Haytham, and Rayan, whose joy, curiosity, and
boundless energy remind me every day why the future is worth securing.*

*To my brothers and sisters, whose early faith in me has always been a quiet
source of strength.*

*May this book reflect the strength of your support and the depth of my
gratitude.*

Contents at a Glance

Contents

Foreword

—by Whitfield Diffie

Cryptography is hardly a new field of endeavor. "Modern cryptography" was conceived twice—in Baghdad 1,200 years ago and in Italy 500 years ago—and born a bit over 100 years ago during World War I. Once we got our teeth into cryptography in the 20th century, it seemed like an important but limited problem, one that might actually be solved. Sure enough, when the U.S. National Security Agency announced its "Suite B" of unclassified algorithms trusted for all levels of classified information, it seemed that the problem might in fact have been solved. Cryptography, however, refused to go away. Information Technology journals and conferences flourished, and new theories and systems continued to appear. More significantly, for our purposes, a threat that had been lurking for more than a decade came to be better and better recognized.

In about 1990, the physicists' promise of quantum computing began to be widely written about. The idea was to compute on what is called a superposition of states in which every variable involved takes every possible value at the same time, a description you would be forgiven for thinking would allow you to do anything in one clock tick. The reality of quantum computing is more complex, but it quickly began to appear that quantum computing, albeit decades off, might make dramatic improvements in a variety of computational problems.

Think about designing a new molecule, whether for a drug or a new structural material. Assembling atoms and molecules into larger molecules isn't an easy process. Imagine a three-dimensional jigsaw puzzle—yes, it may be important to assemble it in just the right order to be able to get the pieces to where you want them to go—in which the pieces are not rigid; they can take on a number of forms, perhaps changing form during the process of assembly.

One of the first applications to be explored seemed more of a threat than a benefit. In 1994, Peter Shor, working at Bell Labs in Providence, New Jersey, developed a quantum-computing algorithm for finding cycles in transformations on finite sets. The obvious application of Shor's algorithm was finding secret cycle lengths in the public-key cryptosystems—called Diffie-Hellman and RSA (Rivest, Shamir, and Adleman) after their inventors—used to secure internet communications.

Quantum computing was not the first new technology of vast interest to cryptanalysts. Over the decades of its existence, NSA has funded a variety of secret computing projects, particularly intended for attacking cryptographic systems it was working to break. Quantum computing, however, was different. On one hand, by the time it came to the NSA's attention, or at least by the time the NSA took it seriously, it was already being widely talked about and studied. There was a limit to how secret it could be kept. On the other hand, the problem was too big to be solved out of the cryptanalytic budget alone. As a result—whatever research was and is being done on quantum-computing-based cryptanalysis— NSA began to work publicly (at least, publicly for the NSA) on securing the cryptographic systems on which U.S. security depends from the quantum-computing threat.

The NSA's plans surfaced in a remarkably impolitic form in an official memo from the Committee on National Security Systems on 11 August 2015:

IAD recognizes that there will be a move, in the not distant future, to a quantum resistant algorithm suite. . . . For those partners and vendors that have not yet made the transition to Suite B algorithms, we recommend not making a significant expenditure to do so at this point . . .

This memo was sure to have infuriated the many allies and partners that the NSA had been pushing to adopt Suite B since its adoption nearly a decade earlier.

Politic or not, the memo signaled the beginning of a period of development of quantum-computing-resistant algorithms. NIST, the National Institute for Standards and Technology, began a project—in the same international-competition style used to develop the Advanced Encryption Standard—to develop new algorithms, a project that came to a major waypoint, although not completion, in August 2024, with the announcement of three new standards—one for key negotiation and two for signature—that were to form the basis of "post-quantum cryptography." In retrospect, the memo, if premature, was correct.

Major revisions of cryptography are not new: there has been one about every 25 years over the past century, beginning with World War I. The challenge of radio was met with electromechanical machines in the 1920s and 1930s; the challenge of high-speed communication was met with electronics in the 1950s and 1960s; and the challenge of scale presented by the internet was met with public-key cryptography and the use of software encryption in the late 20th century. This is different.

At present, there is no quantum computer that can run Shor's algorithm, no quantum computer that presents a threat to internet cryptography. Moreover, appropriately erudite experts can be found to tell us that such a computer is five years off or that it will never happen. New standards and regulations are here, however, and NIST and the NSA have set up a 10-year timetable. By 2035, everything is expected to be post-quantum secure, and everyone responsible for securing information cryptographically—at least, those who work for or contract with the U.S. government—must take this into account.

The quantum-computing transition in cryptography is different from its predecessors in two other interlinked and important ways. The scale of use of cryptography in the world has undergone an unprecedented transition in the past two or three decades. When military organizations were the primary consumers of cryptography—followed by the banks and oil companies—a large purchase of equipment was hundreds of thousands of devices. Today, billions of browsers implement Suite B, a level of cryptographic strength unknown a decade earlier. Joining this change of scale is another issue: this transition in cryptography is public. During previous transitions, parties who were opponents worked independently to improve their own cryptography, typically hoping that their opponents would not achieve equally good results. In previous eras, the systems in use by opposing national and commercial entities were not intended to interoperate. The internet has brought a new phenomenon to networking: rather than being intended for friends to talk to each other, the internet is a network intended for communications between friends and enemies alike.

One thing on which there is likely to be wide agreement is that in an era of cryptographic transition, there will be a profound demand for education. Security officers, programmers, project managers, and policy makers will need to know what has changed—and much has changed—beyond the names of the systems. It is this educational objective at which this book is aimed.

Introduction to Quantum Computing and Its Impact

"Nature isn't classical, dammit, and if you want to make a simulation of nature, you'd better make it quantum mechanical."

—Richard Feynman

This chapter introduces the basics of quantum computing, how it is different from "classical" computing, why that difference is important, and how it is applied to solve some critical problems. We also call out the urgency of action needed on the part of business entities and government agencies to address the impact of one particular use case of quantum computing—factorization.

Evolution of Computing

Human ingenuity and the relentless pursuit of progress have long served as driving forces in the evolution of computing. From the days of the abacus used by the Chinese, Sumerians, and Egyptians to the advent of mechanical computing devices, or calculators, as early as the 17th century, humans have continued to evolve and develop the ability to compute using devices. Charles Babbage (1791–1871), a renowned English mathematician, is often credited with the conceptual design of the modern-day computer.

The advent of vacuum tubes ushered in the transition from mechanical to electronic computing. The Electronic Numerical Integrator and Computer (ENIAC) was the first computer built using vacuum tubes, in 1946. The IBM 603 was the world's first mass-produced electronic calculator, and it used about 300 vacuum tubes in its calculating unit. "To IBM's astonishment, customers liked the 603 and placed orders for it" [1].

Modern computers, also known as classical computers, rapidly came into existence and gained popularity with the invention of transistors. Transistors not only miniaturized the computers but also made them faster, cheaper, and more reliable. Integrated circuits that contained multiple transistors on a single chip further drove miniaturization and adoption. The notion of a personal computer came into existence, and the PC revolution was effectively ushered in during the 1980s and early 1990s. IBM introduced the IBM Personal Computer in 1981, setting the standards for personal computer hardware for years to come. Complementing the hardware, sophisticated software systems also emerged, and the Microsoft MS-DOS operating system and the notion of applications running on MS-DOS further accelerated the adoption and consumption of PCs. Apple developed and released the Macintosh (or Mac) series of hardware and a companion operating system, offering an alternative to MS-DOS and later Windows-based PCs.

The advent of the Internet and increasing connectivity to it changed the face of computing as well as communications. A parallel and very significant development based on this increased and almost ubiquitous connectivity was the development and proliferation of mobile devices. Smartphones capable of communication and computation drove computing into the hands of millions of consumers. Coupled with cloud computing and increased access to reliable connectivity and communication, computing has evolved several orders of magnitude in a very short time. The Internet of Things (IoT) has driven connectivity to billions of devices, and the emergence of significant processing capabilities through Graphics Processing Unit (GPUs) has catapulted capabilities in artificial intelligence (AI).

The current state of computing is marked by unprecedented advancements in processing power, AI, and connectivity, transforming industries and everyday life with smarter, faster, and more interconnected technologies. In the midst of all this progress, a new paradigm of computing has emerged and gained significant ground in recent years. This is *quantum computing*. Quantum computing represents one of the most promising and revolutionary advancements in the field of computing.

Quantum Computing

Quantum computing represents a revolutionary leap in the field of computation, promising to solve problems that are currently intractable for classical computers. By harnessing the principles of quantum mechanics, quantum computers can perform complex calculations at unprecedented speeds. It is a groundbreaking field that promises to reshape the future of technology and problem-solving. Unlike traditional computing, which has driven innovation for decades, quantum computing opens the door to an entirely new way of approaching complex challenges. It holds the potential to dramatically accelerate solutions to problems that today's fastest computers would take years—or even centuries—to solve.

What makes quantum computing so exciting is not just its speed, but its ability to handle complexity. In fields like medicine, finance, energy, and logistics, some problems involve many variables, changing conditions, and structural complexities. Quantum computers are expected to be able to explore these possibilities more efficiently, offering insights and answers that could revolutionize industries.

Imagine being able to design new medicines in a fraction of the time it takes today, or discovering entirely new materials with properties we've never seen. Not only this, but banks and insurance companies could manage risks better, supply chains could be optimized in real time, and climate models could become more accurate and actionable.

Although still in development, quantum computing is attracting major interest from governments, universities, and corporations worldwide. It is widely regarded as one of the most important technological frontiers of the 21st century, and its progress is being closely watched. The full impact of quantum computing may still be a few years away, but the journey that began in the early 2000s has started to accelerate with major breakthroughs and progress milestones achieved and announced on a regular basis. In June 2025, IBM, a leader in quantum computing, announced that it would have the first large-scale, fault-tolerant quantum computer in 2029. Researchers are making steady progress in overcoming obstacles, and businesses are preparing for a future where quantum technology becomes part of everyday operations. Even now, many are beginning to think not just about what quantum computers can do, but how they will change what we consider possible.

Beyond its technical promise, quantum computing represents a shift in mindset. It encourages us to rethink how we approach the world's hardest problems—by embracing uncertainty, exploring multiple paths, and imagining radically different outcomes. Quantum computing has the potential to revolutionize various fields by solving problems that are currently beyond the reach of classical computers (see Figure 1-1) [2].

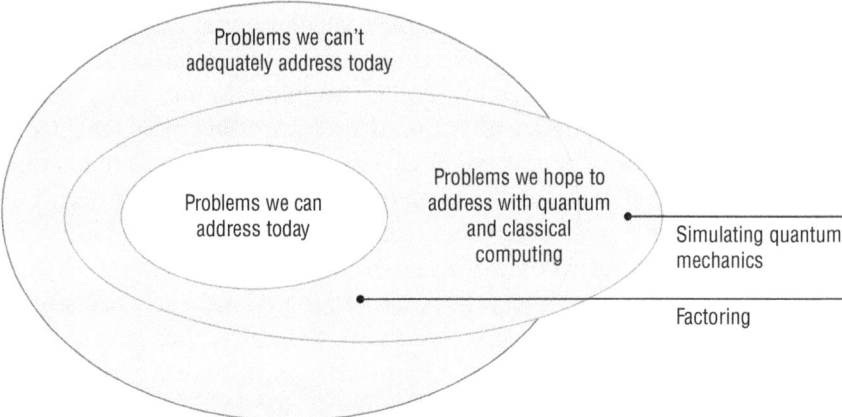

Figure 1-1: Problem domains addressed by computing paradigms

There is a misconception that quantum computers are, in general, faster than classical computers in solving all problems. It is true that quantum computers can solve certain types of problems significantly faster than classical computers, but that does not mean they are faster overall:

- There is a set of problems that classical computers are best suited for and that is not suitable for quantum computers. Multiplication of two numbers is a great example of that.

- There is a set of problems that classical computers cannot solve but quantum computers can. Factorization of an integer is one such problem.

- There is a set of problems that classical computers can solve but quantum computers are much better at solving. Optimization is one such problem.

- There is a set of problems that neither classical nor quantum computers can solve.

Applications of Quantum Computing

As a revolutionary new compute paradigm, quantum computing presents the potential to solve industry problems that were previously very difficult to solve or had to be solved through approximation methods. The field of applied quantum computing is developing quickly, with approaches and algorithms to solve real-world problems across industries. The type of problems that quantum computers solve can be classified into the following categories:

- Chemistry and materials
- Search and optimization
- Mathematical problems

These broad solution areas are developed into specific algorithms and applied to targeted industries to solve real-world problems. Although still in its early stages, quantum computing holds immense promise. As the technology matures, its ability to solve practical challenges will redefine industries and push the boundaries of what computers can achieve. Companies like IBM are working actively with industry, academia, and government to explore quantum computing and apply it in new ways to solve real-world problems and benefit society [2].

The following are some of the potential business applications of quantum computing:

- **Optimization**: Quantum algorithms have the potential to solve complex optimization problems more efficiently, benefiting industries such as logistics, finance, manufacturing, and energy. For example, quantum computing could optimize supply chains, financial portfolios, and traffic flows [3].

- **Numerical simulation**: Quantum computers are used to simulate business scenarios because they offer increased fidelity and the potential to perform significantly more complex simulations than current classical computers can. Monte Carlo simulations on quantum computers have multiple applications, and specialized simulations are used across industries [3].

- **AI**: Quantum algorithms could enhance machine learning and AI. Quantum machine learning (QML) is an emerging field that combines quantum computing with AI to tackle complex data analysis tasks. Optimization of AI models, including improving their performance, reducing training time, and enhancing natural language processing (NLP) tasks, could be a powerful application area of quantum computing [4].

- **Cryptography**: One of the key problems solved by quantum computers is factorization. Factorization and derived math problems are used in classical cryptographic algorithms. Consequently, quantum computers can break classical cryptographic codes, necessitating the development of quantum-safe encryption methods. This is the area of focus of this book; in later chapters, we will detail its impact and approaches to managing this impact effectively [5].

- **Drug discovery**: Quantum computing can simulate molecular interactions at an atomic level, accelerating the discovery of new drugs and materials. This capability could lead to breakthroughs in medicine and materials science [3].

- **Materials science:** Realistic simulation of complex molecules and compounds by quantum computers could lead to the development of new materials with desirable properties. Improving materials used in batteries and developing lighter materials for manufacturing are great examples [3].

- **Healthcare:** Personalized medicine can be developed by applying quantum computing to analyze complex genetic and molecular data. This approach can be used to develop personalized treatment plans tailored to each patient [6].

- **Financial services:** Applying optimization algorithms to various financial services problems, risk analysis, and the development of new trading strategies are other potential areas of impact for quantum computing [3].

- **Telecommunications:** In addition to network optimization approaches, secure communications using quantum key distribution (QKD), a secure communication mechanism based on the principles of quantum mechanics, can prevent hacking or eavesdropping.

- **Weather forecasting:** Due to the ability of quantum computers to process certain complex data, more accurate weather modeling and predictions may be possible [7].

Foundational Concepts of Quantum Computing

Having discussed the advantages of quantum computing and the types of problems it can solve, let's now investigate how a quantum computer differs from its classical counterpart and what the foundational principles of a quantum computer are. Although this information is not essential to the understanding of post-quantum cryptography and its impact, it will provide a level of appreciation for why quantum computers are the next frontier in computing. This will also provide context and a rationale for why the availability of quantum computers that solve business problems is still considered to be years away.

In classical computing, bits of information are represented by either a 0 or a 1. So the value of a bit can be either 0 or 1. These bits can be operated by three basic types of gates: AND, OR, and NOT.

Logic gates operate based on the principles of Boolean algebra:

- An AND gate outputs 1 only when all its inputs are 1.
- An OR gate outputs 1 if at least one of its inputs is 1.
- A NOT gate inverts the input, changing 0 to 1 or 1 to 0.

Logic gates are the foundation of digital computing. By combining these gates, more complex circuits can be created, including multiplexers, registers, arithmetic logic units (ALUs), and even entire microprocessors. Modern microprocessors can contain more than 100 million logic gates, demonstrating their scalability and importance in advanced computing systems.

Quantum computing is based on the foundations of quantum mechanics, the branch of physics that describes the behavior of particles at the smallest scales. Quantum mechanics introduces some concepts that are central to quantum computing:

- **Superposition**: In quantum computing, quantum bits (qubits) can be either 0 or 1 or exist in a superposition of states: that is, they can be in a complex linear combination of 0 and 1 simultaneously. This property allows quantum computers to process a vast number of possibilities at once. See Figure 1-2.

- **Entanglement**: Two qubits can be entangled, and when they are, the state of one qubit is directly related to the state of the other, regardless of the distance that separates them. This phenomenon enables qubits to work together in ways that classical bits cannot, providing a powerful means of parallel computation. See Figure 1-3.

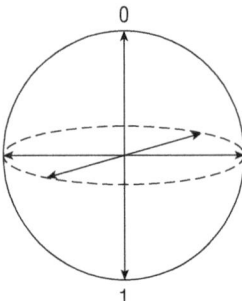

Figure 1-2: Bloch sphere representation of a qubit

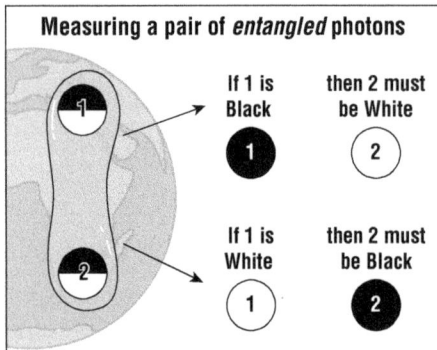

Figure 1-3: Entanglement

- **Interference**: Interference is used to amplify the correct solutions to a problem while canceling out the incorrect ones. This is a key mechanism in many quantum algorithms, leading to faster computations compared to classical approaches. See Figure 1-4.

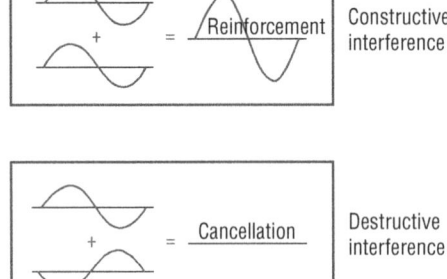

Figure 1-4: Interference

Quantum Gates and Circuits

Quantum computation is performed using quantum gates. A quantum gate is a basic circuit operating on a small set of qubits. These quantum gates are the building blocks of quantum circuits. A quantum circuit is a computing routine that defines a series of logical quantum operations on the underlying qubits. Some of the fundamental quantum gates include the following:

- **Hadamard gate**: Creates an equal superposition state from a basis state, enabling the parallelism of quantum computation. For instance, it takes a qubit from state $|0>$ to a state that is an equal superposition of $|0>$ and $|1>$.

- **CNOT gate**: A two-qubit gate that performs a conditional operation, i.e., flipping the second qubit if the first qubit is $|1\rangle$.

- **Pauli-X gate**: Flips the state of a qubit from $|0\rangle$ to $|1\rangle$ and vice versa. This is analogous to the classical NOT gate.

Quantum circuits are sequences of quantum gates applied to qubits to perform computations. These circuits can solve problems more efficiently than classical circuits for certain tasks [5].

Quantum Hardware

Classical computers operate based on the principles of binary logic, where data is processed using bits that represent either 0 or 1. The architecture of a classical computer follows the von Neumann architecture, which consists of key components, including the central processing unit (CPU), memory, storage, input/output devices, and buses that facilitate communication between these components. Classical computers are deterministic, meaning that repeating the same input always yields the same output. They operate on bits and are based on Boolean algebra, contrasting with quantum computers, which use qubits and operate probabilistically. The architecture of classical computers has been proven to be robust, and it remains the backbone of current-day computing systems.

Rather than classical logic, quantum computers use matrix operations that yield probabilistic outputs based on quantum mechanical principles. However, the quantum states into which the information is encoded are extremely vulnerable to noise from the system and the environment. Although error correction at scale has not yet been achieved, multiple companies and research groups are investigating and developing different types of qubits and quantum computer architectures in the hopes of making quantum computing commercially viable.

Several physical implementations of qubits are being explored, each with its own advantages and limitations:

- **Superconducting qubits**: These qubits use superconducting circuits cooled to near absolute zero. They are currently the most mature technology and are used by companies like IBM and Google in their quantum processors.

- **Quantum dot qubits**: These are nanoparticles made of a semiconductor material. Each one is usually a free electron isolated within a sphere inside a solid. This free electron is held in place and switched on or off using electrical fields.

- **Trapped ions**: Individual ions, atoms that have lost or gained an electron, are trapped and manipulated using electromagnetic fields. This approach offers high coherence times and is being pursued by companies like IonQ and academic research groups.

- **Topological qubits**: Based on exotic states of matter, topological qubits are designed to be more resistant to errors. Microsoft is a key player in researching this approach.

- **Photonic qubits**: Using photons as qubits offers the advantage of room-temperature operation and easy integration with existing communication technologies. Companies like Xanadu are exploring this technology [8].

The most promising of these approaches seems to be superconducting qubits, with leaders such as IBM making rapid strides in recent years and deploying more than 75 quantum computers on the cloud for users to access based on this technology [9, p. 71].

Challenges in Developing Quantum Computers

Advancements in quantum computing face several technical challenges. These need to be solved before a scalable and reliable quantum computer can be built that can solve real business problems:

- **Decoherence**: Qubits are highly sensitive to noise in their surroundings. When a qubit loses its quantum state due to such noise, it is said to *decohere*. Decoherence can be due to noise such as electromagnetic signals, temperature fluctuations, vibrations, etc. The result of this is data loss and computational errors.

- **Error rates**: Qubits are also prone to errors due to noise and instability. The result is an inability to perform long-term computations.

- **Error correction at scale**: Robust techniques that can mitigate or correct these errors at production scale are necessary so that robust quantum computers can be built.

Building a quantum computer that could break modern cryptographic algorithms—or what is known as a cryptographically relevant quantum computer (CRQC)—requires a high level of scalability, i.e., millions of qubits with low error rates and long coherence times.

Quantum Algorithms

The various business applications of quantum computing mentioned in the previous section are primarily based on applying a set of fundamental or foundational algorithms. These quantum algorithms leverage the principles of quantum mechanics to solve specific problems faster than classical algorithms.

Some of these algorithms are as follows:

- **Shor's algorithm**: Developed by Peter Shor in 1994, when no usable quantum computer was available, this algorithm demonstrates how large numbers can be factorized exponentially faster than the best-known classical algorithms. Its potential to break widely used cryptographic codes has significant implications for cybersecurity [5].

- **Grover's algorithm**: This algorithm, designed by Lov Grover in 1996, provides a faster way to execute a search in unstructured datasets. The speedup offered is quadratic, not exponential, as in the case of Shor's algorithm. But this algorithm offers significant performance improvements for certain tasks [5].

- **Quantum Fourier transform (QFT)**: Execution of Fourier transforms is an essential component of many quantum algorithms. QFT is an efficient computational approach for the discrete Fourier transform of quantum states. It is a critical component of Shor's algorithm and other quantum algorithms [5].

Quantum Computing and Modern Cryptography

As we have seen in the previous section, quantum computing offers solutions to several intractable problems, which in turn have far-reaching positive business impacts and deliver benefits across various industries and disciplines. At the same time, a powerful quantum computer in the hands of bad actors has the potential to cause significant harm and damage. Such a use case lies at the intersection of quantum computing and current-day cryptography.

We introduce the problem in this chapter. Chapter 3 offers an in-depth treatment of classical cryptography and its applications, as well as new cryptographic algorithms that are safe from attacks orchestrated by either classical or quantum computers.

Modern cryptography uses three types of cryptographic algorithms:

- Asymmetric cryptographic algorithms
- Symmetric cryptographic algorithms
- Hashing algorithms

Asymmetric cryptographic algorithms use factorization or logarithmic problems as their basis. These cannot be solved by the fastest supercomputers that exist today, even in a million years. However, as pointed out earlier, a CRQC can solve factorization problems by applying Shor's algorithm in a matter of hours or days.

Symmetric cryptography and hashing algorithms can be broken by applying Grover's algorithm. Because Grover's algorithm offers only a quadratic speedup, the risk is not as severe as that faced by asymmetric cryptography-based algorithms.

Because asymmetric algorithms could be broken, public key encryption, digital signatures, and key exchange algorithms are all at risk. By extension, asymmetric cryptography protocols such as Rivest-Shamir-Adleman (RSA), digital signature algorithm (DSA), elliptic curve cryptography (ECC), elliptic curve digital signature algorithm (ECDSA), and Diffie-Hellman (DH) could potentially be broken by a CRQC.

In short, when a CRQC becomes available, all digital communications based on asymmetric cryptography will be vulnerable, posing a significant threat to cybersecurity.

Impact of Potential Threats to Modern Cryptography

Every digital interaction, from texting friends and family, online banking, making travel reservations, and securing critical infrastructure to inter-enterprise exchanges, and so on, is based on trust—trust that our interactions are indeed secure. That trust and security are based on cryptography. Cryptography is often referred to as the last line of digital defense.

Cryptography touches every corner of the digital world. Some illustrative samples of the digital world are as follows:

- **Internet**: Cryptography is part of commonly used protocols that make up the Internet, such as Domain Name Service (DNS), Hypertext Transfer Protocol (HTTP), Telnet, and File Transfer Protocol (FTP).

- **Critical infrastructure**: Software that manages electrical grids, critical control systems, control systems embedded into automobiles, etc., are all driven by software that depends on encryption and cryptography for its confidential data exchange.

- **Financial systems**: Beyond consumer financial systems, such as banking transactions, financial trades made online, and digital payments effected through mechanisms such as Venmo and PayPal, enterprise-scale payment systems (Fedwire, EMV, TARGET2, etc.), SWIFT, and other settlement systems all depend on security offered by cryptography.

- **Blockchain**: Blockchain-based systems, their authentication, and instruments such as wallets, ledgers, and transactions all depend on secure encryption of data and their exchange.

- **Enterprise IT**: The backbone of enterprise communication in our current digital world depends on cryptography: email; systems used by enterprises to authenticate and authorize users, such as LDAP services; and virus-scanning systems that ensure the safety and security of data.

It is safe to say that almost all systems and applications that we use daily and take for granted depend on the security offered by digital cryptography and are likely to be compromised by a CRQC. Even though there have been significant advancements in quantum computing over the past decade or so, we do not yet have a quantum computer that can break such encryption. This leads to the following questions:

- What is being done to ensure that our digital communications continue to be safe?
- When will a CRQC be available?
- What can a bad actor do by breaking cryptography?
- Why is there need for concern now?

We will provide a short synopsis of the answers here. The rest of the book is dedicated to answering these questions and more in depth.

Ensuring the Continued Safety of Digital Communications

Anticipating the developments in quantum computing and the impending potential of a CRQC breaking modern-day cryptography, the National Institute of Standards and Technology (NIST) started conducting competitions and soliciting submissions for cryptographic algorithms that cannot be broken by either classical or quantum computers. These algorithms are called post-quantum cryptography (PQC).

Competitions conducted since 2016 have resulted in NIST announcing the selection of four algorithms around which standards will be built and publishing the standards for three of the four algorithms. These are ready for consumption. These algorithms are based on a variety of challenging math problems that cannot be solved by classical or quantum computers, such as learning with errors (LWE), finding short vectors in nth-degree truncated polynomial ring units (NTRU), multivariate quadratic equations, and isogeny. We talk more about these algorithms in the next chapter.

Additional submissions have been invited for targeted, special-purpose algorithms, which will be scrutinized, evaluated, and tested. Those selected will also result in the publication of standards. In short, additional algorithms can be expected in the coming months and years.

So, the answer to the question of what is being done to ensure that our digital communications continue to be safe is that PQC algorithms are being certified by NIST. The current set of asymmetric cryptography-based algorithms should eventually be replaced with appropriate PQC algorithms.

Availability of a CRQC

Although no one can predict when a quantum computer capable of breaking encryption will become available, we can look at several data points and arrive at an estimate. Some critical data points are as follows:

- NIST estimates that RSA-2048 may be broken as early as 2030 [10].

- National security memoranda (NSM-8 and NSM-10) communicate the urgency of getting started on the PQC transition and transformation [11].

- A Commercial National Security Algorithm (CNSA) 2.0 advisory from the National Security Agency in the United States has laid out a timeline for national security systems to be PQC compliant by 2033 [12].

- A study conducted by the World Economic Forum concluded that quantum computers are likely to break cryptography in the early 2030s (2030 to 2035) [13].

- Studies from the analyst firm Gartner called out that cryptography could be broken as early as 2028 [14].

- A joint announcement by IBM, Google, the University of Chicago, and the University of Tokyo estimates that a 100,000-qubit quantum computer is likely viable by 2030.

Based on these data points and other studies conducted by industry analysts and estimates offered by quantum experts in the field, it is reasonable to estimate that a CRQC will be available in the early 2030s.

Actions of Bad Actors

The threat of what a bad actor can do with a quantum computer is here now, but its impact will be felt much later. That is, the threat exists today, but the impact will happen tomorrow.

The actions and impact of what a bad actor can do are measured across two time frames:

- Between now and when a CRQC becomes available
- After a CRQC becomes available

Bad actors can exfiltrate encrypted data today without any means of decrypting it, even without knowing whether it contains sensitive information or is otherwise valuable. They can wait until a CRQC becomes available, decrypt what they have exfiltrated now, and potentially exploit the sensitivity and value of the data to cause harm. This is called *harvest now and decrypt later*. Almost everyone is exposed to this threat today, and unfortunately, there is neither a way to detect it nor a way to protect data that has already been exfiltrated.

In the future, when a CRQC becomes available, in addition to decrypting harvested data and causing damage, bad actors will be able to actively decrypt classic cryptography-based encryption and perform fraudulent authentication; create fake identities; forge digital signatures; masquerade as someone they are not; launch extortion attacks by threatening to disclose harvested data; and create indistinguishable fraudulent documents such as land ownership documents, lease documents, etc.

Essentially, the final line of defense protecting our digital assets will be breached, causing irreparable harm and global loss of value beyond estimation.

Need for Action Now

With a CRQC not likely to be a reality until in the early 2030s, you may wonder why enterprises should be concerned about it today. The main reasons are the potential long-term implications for data security, the overall complexity of transitioning to quantum-safe systems, regulatory requirements, and the potential competitive advantage.

Data Longevity

We have seen that sensitive data encrypted today could be at risk in the future when quantum computers become capable of breaking current encryption. In industries where data needs to be protected for decades, this issue is very profound and requires critical consideration.

Take healthcare as an example: patient data, personalized treatment information, drug-discovery-related information, clinical trial data, and so on have a time value well beyond 10 years. Tax records in most countries must be retained for 7–10 years. Industry regulations may also require the retention of records for 10 years or more. Military secrets, passport information, intellectual-property-related information, and patents are all types of data with a longer time value. Hence, protecting all this information becomes a critical priority today.

Complexity of Transition

The use of cryptography is pervasive in the enterprise landscape and in almost all applications currently in use. However, no one in an enterprise has a comprehensive inventory of all such cryptographic usage.

This is because the use of cryptography in software systems began as early as the late 1970s with the discovery of the DH protocol in 1976 and the RSA protocol in 1977. Since then, applications have grown organically in size and complexity, as well as in their use of cryptography. Organizations have grown through acquisitions, and along with these acquisitions came additional software components. Organizations also started consuming third-party software by way of commercial off-the-shelf software (COTS), web services offered by their ecosystem partners, and cloud services essential for their business. Consequently, there is no comprehensive inventory of cryptography being used by enterprises across all these systems, applications, services, and other components.

Transitioning to PQC requires identifying every instance of current classic cryptography usage and applying appropriate remediation approaches so they become quantum safe. This is by no means a trivial effort. On the contrary, it requires meticulous preparation and thoughtful, iterative execution. Earlier cryptographic transitions, such as moving from Secure Hash Algorithm 1 (SHA-1) to Secure Hash Algorithm 2 (SHA-2) or from Data Encryption Standard (DES) to Advanced Encryption Standard (AES), which were relatively smaller in scope, have taken anywhere from 7 to 10 years to complete. Many enterprises have yet to complete this exercise.

In addition, updating hardware systems embedded in IoT devices, aircraft, trains, automobiles, and other critical infrastructure components requires several years of lead time, planning, and execution.

This is not just about systems in an enterprise's control being upgraded to be quantum safe. Although that is necessary, it is not sufficient. All ecosystem partners, third-party software providers, and so on need to upgrade their systems and become quantum safe, or PQC-compliant, as well. In other words, the entire software supply chain of the enterprise must become quantum safe.

Other influencing considerations are the following:

- **Regulatory requirements**: Governments and regulatory bodies are likely to mandate quantum-safe encryption standards. Preparing now can help enterprises stay ahead of compliance requirements and avoid potential fines or penalties and damage to reputation.

▪ **Competitive advantage**: Being an early adopter of quantum-safe technologies can position enterprises as leaders in cybersecurity, enhance their reputation, and provide them with first-mover advantages.

Preparing for the quantum computing era is a strategic necessity for enterprises to ensure long-term data security and maintain a competitive edge. By taking proactive steps beginning now, enterprises can effectively mitigate the risks posed by future quantum computers and ensure a smooth transition to quantum-safe cryptography.

Responsible Quantum Computing

As we have seen, several potentially significant developments can be made by the responsible application of quantum computing capabilities. These can have a very positive impact on our society and deliver overall benefits for all. However, we have also seen that bad actors can cause significant damage by irresponsible use of quantum computing capabilities. This demands a set of guidelines and principles to govern the responsible use of quantum computing. Although such responsible quantum computing principles are in their infancy, the following starter set may develop into a robust set of guidelines in the future [15]:

▪ Focus on use cases that make a positive societal impact.

▪ Anticipate unintended impacts of use cases that seem positive.

▪ Represent quantum's promises and limitations appropriately.

▪ Demonstrate consistency and transparency in decisions.

▪ Build an inclusive quantum ecosystem that represents the diversity of the world at large.

Summary

Quantum computing presents the next frontier in computing. It will not replace classical computing; rather, it will exist alongside classical computer systems. Quantum computing offers the potential of breakthrough solutions to some intractable problems that exist today. Although these breakthroughs will yield significant advantages when available and advance solutions across many industries, one of the use cases of quantum computing—namely, factorization—has the potential to break current-day cryptography.

This poses a significant threat to the trust upon which our digital economy relies. It has pushed standards bodies like NIST to source, scrutinize, select, and publish post-quantum cryptography (PQC)-based algorithms that enterprises should begin to adopt.

Enterprises should begin adopting PQC now because of the "harvest now, decrypt later" phenomenon: data with a time value of over 7 to 10 years needs to be protected today. In addition, the pervasiveness of cryptography usage and the inherent complexity of remediating classic cryptography will require anywhere from 7 to 10 years to complete an effective transition to become quantum safe.

This chapter has also highlighted a critical aspect of quantum computing: guidelines for responsible quantum computing.

References

(1) K. Maney, *The Maverick and His Machine*, Thomas Watson, Sr. and the Making of IBM.

(2) J. D. Hidary, *Quantum Computing: An Applied Approach*, Springer, 2019.

(3) IBM Institute of Business Value, Quantum Decade, 2023.

(4) Quantum Computers Will Make AI Better, 2025, https://www.quantinuum.com/blog/quantum-computers-will-make-ai-better.

(5) R. S. Sutor, *Dancing with Qubits*, Packt, 2019.

(6) IBM, Exploring quantum computing use cases for healthcare, 2023, https://www.ibm.com/thought-leadership/institute-business-value/en-us/report/quantum-healthcare.

(7) M. Swayne, Study Explores Hybrid Quantum Algorithms for Improved Weather Prediction, Climate Modeling, Quantum Insider, 2024, https://thequantuminsider.com/2024/10/21/study-explores-hybrid-quantum-algorithms-for-improved-weather-prediction-climate-modeling.

(8) D. A. Ray, 7 Primary Qubit Technologies for Quantum Computing, 2018, `https://amitray.com/` `7-core-qubit-technologies-for-quantum-computing/#` `Quantumdotsqubits`.

(9) IBM, Investor Day briefing, 2025, `https://www.ibm.com/` `downloads/documents/us-en/11ed328699d6e994`.

(10) NIST, Report on Post-Quantum Cryptography, 2016, `https://` `csrc.nist.gov/files/pubs/ir/8105/final/docs/` `nistir_8105_draft.pdf`.

(11) The White House, National Security Memorandum on Promoting United States Leadership in Quantum Computing While Mitigating Risks to Vulnerable Cryptographic Systems, 2022, `https://bidenwhitehouse.archives.gov/briefing-room/` `statements-releases/2022/05/04/national-security-` `memorandum-on-promoting-united-states-leadership-in-` `quantum-computing-while-mitigating-risks-to-vulnerable-` `cryptographic-systems`.

(12) National Security Agency, 2023, `https://www.nsa.gov/Resources/` `Multimedia/igphoto/2003071761`.

(13) World Economic Forum, `https://reports.weforum.org/docs/` `WEF_Global_Cybersecurity_Outlook_2025.pdf`, 2025.

(14) M. Horvath, Begin transitioning to post-quantum cryptography now, 2024, `https://www.gartner.com/en/articles/` `post-quantum-cryptography`.

(15) IBM, Responsible quantum computing, `https://docs.quantum` `.ibm.com/responsible-quantum-computing`.

Cryptography: An Ultimate Line of Defense for the Digital World

"Cryptography is about mathematical guarantees for information security."
—Shafi Goldwasser

In an era defined by digital transformation and rising cyber threats, cryptography stands as the ultimate line of defense for protecting sensitive data, preserving privacy, and ensuring trust. This chapter provides business and technology leaders with a strategic and practical understanding of cryptography, from its historical roots to modern-day applications and quantum-resistant innovations. Readers will gain clarity on essential encryption techniques, key management challenges, regulatory expectations, and real-world use cases across industries. With a focus on actionable insights and future-ready strategies, this chapter equips leaders to confidently architect cryptographic resilience, drive compliance, and lead their organizations on a pragmatic journey toward becoming quantum safe.

Introduction to Cryptography and Its Importance

Cryptography, derived from the Greek words "kryptos" (meaning hidden) and "graphein" (meaning writing), is the practice of securing information through encoding. It ensures that only authorized parties can access or understand the information. The primary objective of cryptography is to protect data confidentiality, integrity, and authenticity [1].

The history of cryptography dates to ancient civilizations, where simple techniques like the Caesar cipher were used for secret communication. Julius Caesar used this substitution cipher to protect military messages, shifting letters by a fixed number of positions. Over time, cryptography has evolved into a sophisticated field, encompassing a range of techniques and methodologies that have become integral to securing modern digital communications.

In the Middle Ages, cryptography saw advances with the development of polyalphabetic ciphers, such as the Vigenère cipher, which offered more complexity and resistance to frequency analysis attacks. The 20th century introduced mechanical and electromechanical encryption devices, such as the Enigma machine, which was used extensively during World War II. The work of cryptanalysts in breaking these codes marked a significant turning point in the field.

With the advent of computers in the latter half of the 20th century, cryptography entered the digital age. The first official encryption standard called Data Encryption Standard (DES) was based on IBM's 'Lucifer' cipher developed in 1970s and then published as Federal Information Processing Standard (FIPS) in 1977 by National Bureau of Standards (NBS), predecessor to National Institute of Standards and Technology (NIST). DES became the first widely implemented symmetric algorithm for U.S. federal data protection, laying groundwork—but its 56-bit key is now too short for modern security. In 1976, Whitfield Diffie and Martin Hellman revolutionized the field by introducing the first practical method for secure communication over unsecured channels without prior shared secrets—established foundation for public-key cryptography, and shortly thereafter Rivest, Shamir, and Adleman published the first practical RSA algorithm in 1977, enabling encryption and digital signatures without pre-shared secrets [2].

Relevance in Today's Digital Age

In today's digital age, cryptography is more relevant than ever. As businesses, governments, and individuals increasingly rely on digital platforms for communication, transactions, and data storage, the need to protect sensitive information from unauthorized access and cyber threats has become paramount. Cryptography plays a crucial role in safeguarding personal information, financial transactions, intellectual property, and national security.

The rise of cybercrime, data breaches, and identity theft has highlighted the importance of robust cryptographic solutions. Cryptography ensures that sensitive data remains confidential and tamper-proof even if intercepted by malicious actors. It also provides mechanisms for authentication, verifying the identity of users and devices involved in digital interactions.

Furthermore, cryptography underpins the security of emerging technologies such as blockchain, the Internet of Things (IoT), and cloud computing. In blockchain, cryptographic techniques enable secure and transparent transactions without a central authority. In IoT, cryptography ensures the privacy and integrity of data exchanged between connected devices. In cloud computing, cryptography protects data stored and processed in remote servers, addressing concerns about unauthorized access and data loss or theft.

The Evolution of Cryptographic Techniques

Cryptographic techniques have evolved significantly over the years, driven by advancements in technology and the increasing complexity of cyber threats. Early cryptographic methods were primarily focused on obfuscation, relying on the secrecy of the algorithm itself. However, modern cryptography emphasizes the use of publicly known algorithms and the secrecy of cryptographic keys.

Symmetric encryption, where the same key is used for both encryption and decryption, was the foundation of early cryptographic systems. However, its reliance on secure key distribution posed challenges, especially in large-scale networks. Asymmetric encryption, introduced with public-key cryptography, addressed this issue by using a pair of keys—public and private—for encryption and decryption. While asymmetric algorithms remove the need for pre-shared secrets, they are computationally intensive; in practice, they are used to securely exchange symmetric session keys, which then encrypt bulk data efficiently [1].

The development of cryptographic hash functions, digital signatures, and key exchange protocols further expanded the capabilities of cryptography. Hash functions provide a way to verify data integrity by generating a unique fingerprint for each dataset. Digital signatures offer a means of authenticating the origin and integrity of digital messages or documents. Key exchange protocols enable two parties to agree on a session key over an unsecured channel.

Recent advancements in cryptography focus on post-quantum cryptography, which aims to develop algorithms resistant to quantum computing attacks. Quantum computers have the potential to break traditional cryptographic algorithms, posing a significant threat to current encryption standards. Post-quantum cryptography seeks to address this challenge by designing algorithms that remain secure even in the presence of quantum adversaries [3].

Cryptography Primer for Business

In the modern enterprise landscape, cryptography is no longer confined to the realm of security engineers and mathematicians. Business leaders, product managers, and risk officers must now understand the implications of cryptographic technologies to make informed strategic decisions. This primer introduces essential concepts in symmetric and asymmetric encryption, demystifies key management, and provides an overview of public-key infrastructure (PKI). It empowers nontechnical leaders with the knowledge necessary to evaluate security architectures, engage in vendor assessments, and participate in policy development that aligns with business goals and regulatory requirements [1].

Basic Concepts: Symmetric vs. Asymmetric Encryption

Symmetric encryption, also known as secret-key encryption, is a cryptographic technique that uses the same key for both encryption and decryption. It is fast and efficient, making it suitable for encrypting large amounts of data. However, its main challenge lies in secure key distribution and management. If the key is compromised, the confidentiality of the encrypted data is at risk.

Common symmetric encryption algorithms include the following:

- **Advanced Encryption Standard (AES):** AES is a widely adopted symmetric encryption standard known for its strength and efficiency. It supports key sizes of 128, 192, and 256 bits, offering robust security for various applications.

- **Data Encryption Standard (DES):** Once a standard for encryption, DES is now considered obsolete due to its relatively short key length of 56 bits, making it vulnerable to brute-force attacks. It has been largely replaced by AES.

- **Triple DES (3DES):** An enhancement of DES, 3DES applies the DES algorithm three times with different keys, increasing its security. However, it is slower than AES and not as widely used today.

Asymmetric encryption, or public-key encryption, uses a pair of keys—a public key for encryption and a private key for decryption. The public key is openly shared, and the private key remains confidential to the owner. This approach eliminates the need for secure key distribution, making it ideal for securing communications over the internet [3].

Key advantages of asymmetric encryption include the following:

- **Key exchange:** Asymmetric encryption enables secure exchange of symmetric keys, which can then be used for fast encryption of data.

- **Digital signatures:** It allows the creation of digital signatures, providing authentication and integrity verification for digital messages and documents.

These are two common asymmetric encryption algorithms:

- **RSA (Rivest-Shamir-Adleman):** RSA is one of the most widely used public-key encryption algorithms. It relies on the mathematical properties of large prime numbers and supports both encryption and digital signatures.

- **Elliptic curve cryptography (ECC):** ECC is a more recent approach to public-key cryptography, offering security like RSA with smaller key sizes. This efficiency makes it suitable for resource-constrained environments, such as IoT devices.

Hash functions and digital signature algorithms also play critical role in modern cryptography. Hash functions ensure data integrity by generating fixed-length outputs that uniquely represent input data, while digital signature algorithms provide a way to verify the authenticity and origin of digital messages. Together, they help secure communications, protect data, and build trust in digital systems.

Hash functions:

- **SHA-256 (Secure Hash Algorithm 256-bit):** A 256-bit cryptographic hash from the SHA-2 family, widely used for integrity and digital signatures; collision-resistant and secure.

- **SHA-3 family:** Standardized in 2015, SHA-3 uses a sponge construction with different cryptographic foundations, offering resilience against length-extension and collision attacks.

- **MD5 and SHA-1:** Both hash functions are deprecated due to proven collision vulnerabilities; unsuitable for digital signatures or secure integrity verification.

Digital Signature Algorithms:

- **DSA (Digital Signature Algorithm):** DSA is a standard digital signature algorithm used to verify the authenticity and integrity of digital messages and documents.

- **ECDSA (Elliptic Curve Digital Signature Algorithm):** ECDSA is an elliptic curve variant of DSA, offering similar security with smaller key sizes.

Key Management: Challenges and Best Practices

Key management is a critical aspect of cryptographic systems, encompassing the generation, distribution, storage, rotation, and revocation of cryptographic keys. Effective key management ensures the security and integrity of encrypted data [4, 5].

Effective key management is the backbone of any secure cryptographic system. Without strong controls around how keys are generated, distributed, stored, and retired, even the most advanced encryption algorithms can be rendered ineffective. Organizations must address several operational and technical challenges to ensure that cryptographic keys remain secure throughout their lifecycle. These challenges include the following:

- **Secure key generation:** Generating cryptographic keys with sufficient entropy and randomness is essential to prevent predictability and vulnerabilities.

- **Key distribution:** Distributing keys securely to authorized parties without exposing them to interception or unauthorized access is a significant challenge, especially in large-scale environments.

- **Key storage:** Storing keys securely is vital to prevent unauthorized access. Keys should be protected using hardware security modules (HSMs) or secure key vaults.

- **Key rotation:** Regularly rotating keys minimizes the risk of long-term exposure. However, key rotation must be managed carefully to avoid data access disruptions.

- **Key revocation:** In cases of key compromise or employee turnover, revoking keys promptly is crucial to prevent unauthorized access to encrypted data.

To maintain the integrity and confidentiality of encrypted data, organizations must adopt disciplined and proactive key management practices. The following best practices help ensure cryptographic keys are handled securely throughout their lifecycle:

- **Use strong key lengths.** Longer keys provide greater security against brute-force attacks. Organizations should use key lengths recommended by industry standards, such as AES-256 for symmetric encryption and 2048-bit or higher for RSA.

- **Implement key hierarchies.** Using key hierarchies allows for efficient key management by organizing keys into different levels with specific roles and responsibilities.

- **Utilize HSMs.** HSMs provide a secure environment for key generation, storage, and cryptographic operations, protecting keys from unauthorized access and tampering.

- **Regularly audit and monitor keys.** Conduct regular audits of key management practices and monitor key usage to detect and respond to potential security incidents.

- **Educate employees.** Training employees on key management policies and best practices is essential to minimize human errors and insider threats.

Public-Key Infrastructure (PKI)

PKI is a framework that enables secure communication and authentication over the Internet using public-key cryptography. It involves a set of technologies, policies, and procedures for creating, distributing, managing, and revoking digital certificates and public–private key pairs [1].

PKI is built on a structured set of components that work together to establish, manage, and revoke digital trust. Understanding these core building blocks is essential for implementing secure communications and identity verification at scale:

- **Certificate authority (CA):** The CA is a trusted entity responsible for issuing and revoking digital certificates. It verifies the identity of entities requesting certificates and signs them with its private key.

- **Registration authority (RA):** The RA acts as an intermediary between the user and the CA, verifying the user's identity before forwarding the certificate request to the CA.

- **Digital certificates:** Digital certificates bind a public key to the identity of the certificate holder, providing a means of verifying authenticity in digital communications.

- **Certificate revocation list (CRL):** The CRL is a list of revoked certificates, indicating that they should no longer be trusted. It is regularly updated by the CA.

- **Public and private keys:** PKI relies on public–private key pairs for encryption, decryption, and digital signatures. The public key is shared openly, and the private key remains confidential.

By enabling encryption, authentication, and digital signatures, PKI supports a wide range of real-world security use cases that are critical to business operations. Key examples include the following:

- **Secure email communication:** PKI enables secure email communication by encrypting messages and verifying the sender's identity using digital signatures.

- **TLS for websites:** PKI is fundamental to the Transport Layer Security (TLS) protocol, securing data transmitted between web browsers and servers.

- **Authentication and access control:** PKI is used for user authentication in various applications, ensuring that only authorized users can access sensitive resources.

- **Code signing:** PKI is employed to sign software code, verifying its authenticity and integrity to protect against tampering and malware.

Real-World Application Scenarios

Cryptography is essential for securing various business applications and processes. Here are some real-world scenarios where cryptographic techniques play a vital role:

- **Secure online transactions:** Cryptography ensures the security of online transactions by encrypting sensitive payment information, such as credit card numbers, during transmission.

- **Data protection in cloud services:** Encryption protects data stored and processed in cloud environments, ensuring confidentiality and compliance with privacy regulations.

- **Virtual private networks (VPNs):** VPNs use encryption to create secure tunnels for transmitting data over public networks, safeguarding remote access to corporate resources.

- **Secure messaging applications:** End-to-end encryption in messaging apps ensures that only the intended recipients can read the messages, preventing eavesdropping.

- **Digital identity verification:** Cryptography enables secure verification of digital identities, facilitating secure access to online services and applications.

- **Blockchain and cryptocurrency:** Cryptographic techniques underpin blockchain technology, ensuring the integrity and security of transactions in decentralized networks.

Understanding the Pervasiveness of Encryption Across Business Security, Privacy, and Compliance

Encryption is not an isolated technical feature—it permeates every layer of digital business infrastructure, from application development to customer interaction and regulatory adherence. This section highlights how encryption contributes to enterprise security, ensures data privacy, and supports compliance with a growing landscape of legal mandates. As encryption becomes a central pillar of trust in digital ecosystems, leaders must recognize its operational, ethical, and strategic importance in managing information risks and upholding reputational value [3].

Role of Encryption in Data Security

Encryption is a fundamental component of data security, providing a robust mechanism to protect sensitive information from unauthorized access and cyber threats. By converting plaintext data into ciphertext, encryption ensures that even if data is intercepted or accessed without authorization, it remains unreadable and unusable. Figure 2-1 shows the benefits of encryption.

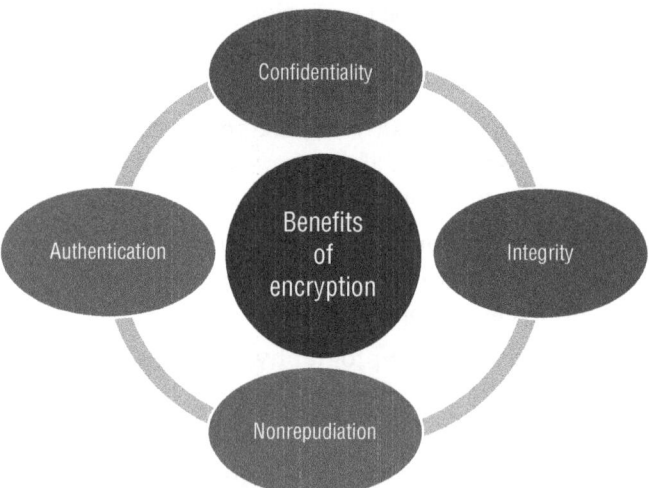

Figure 2-1: Benefits of encryption

Key benefits of encryption in data security include the following:

- **Confidentiality:** Encryption ensures that sensitive data is accessible only to authorized parties with the decryption key.
- **Integrity:** Cryptographic hash functions verify data integrity by detecting any unauthorized modifications or tampering.
- **Authentication:** Digital signatures provide a means of verifying the authenticity and identity of data sources.
- **Nonrepudiation:** Digital signatures also offer nonrepudiation, preventing entities from denying their involvement in digital transactions.

Ensuring Privacy with Encryption

Privacy is a critical concern for businesses handling sensitive customer information. Encryption plays a vital role in protecting privacy by safeguarding personal data and ensuring compliance with data protection regulations.

Key considerations for ensuring privacy with encryption include the following:

- **Data minimization:** A privacy and security principle that means collecting, using, and storing only the minimum amount of personal data necessary to achieve a specific purpose.

- **End-to-end encryption:** Implementing end-to-end encryption ensures that data remains encrypted throughout its lifecycle, from creation to storage and transmission.

- **Anonymization and pseudonymization:** Encryption can be used to anonymize or pseudonymize data, protecting individual identities while allowing data analysis.

- **Secure data sharing:** Encryption enables secure data sharing with third parties, ensuring that privacy is maintained even when data is transferred outside the organization.

Regulatory Compliance and Standards

Regulatory compliance is a significant driver for the adoption of encryption in businesses. Various regulations mandate the use of encryption to protect sensitive data and ensure privacy.

Key regulations and standards include the following:

- **General Data Protection Regulation (GDPR):** GDPR requires organizations to implement appropriate technical and organizational measures, including encryption, to protect the personal data of EU residents [6].

- **Health Insurance Portability and Accountability Act (HIPAA):** HIPAA mandates the use of encryption to protect electronic protected health information (ePHI) and ensure patient privacy [7].

- **Payment Card Industry Data Security Standard (PCI DSS):** PCI DSS requires the use of encryption to protect payment card data during transmission and storage [8].

- **Federal Information Processing Standards (FIPS):** FIPS is a set of several cybersecurity standards for including cryptographic modules used by federal agencies to ensure data security [3].

Case Studies: Data Breaches and How Encryption Could Have Mitigated the Impact

Examining real-world data breaches highlights the importance of encryption in mitigating the impact of security incidents.

Case Study 1: MOVEit Data Breach (2023)

- **Incident:** A critical zero-day vulnerability in the MOVEit file-transfer software allowed threat actors to access sensitive data from over 2,000 organizations, affecting at least 60 million individuals worldwide.

- **Impact:** The incident led to significant operational disruption, regulatory scrutiny, class-action lawsuits, and severe reputational damage across healthcare, financial, and governmental sectors.

- **Mitigation:** Comprehensive end-to-end encryption (E2EE) of files both at rest and in transit could have significantly reduced the breach's impact by rendering sensitive data unintelligible, even after unauthorized access.

Case Study 2: Colonial Pipeline Ransomware Attack (2021)

- **Incident:** A ransomware attack compromised Colonial Pipeline's operational technology and billing systems, forcing the shutdown of a major fuel pipeline and disrupting fuel supply on the U.S. East Coast.

- **Impact:** The attack caused widespread fuel shortages, consumer panic buying, significant economic impact, and payment of a $4.4 million ransom.

- **Mitigation:** Encrypting sensitive operational and billing data at rest and in transit could have prevented unauthorized access and exfiltration, rendering stolen information unusable to attackers and reducing the risk of regulatory penalties and reputational harm.

Case Study 3: Equifax data breach (2017)

- **Incident:** The Equifax data breach exposed sensitive personal information, including Social Security numbers, of approximately 147 million individuals.

- **Impact:** The breach led to significant financial and reputational damage for Equifax, along with legal and regulatory consequences.

- **Mitigation:** Proper encryption of sensitive data, both in transit and at rest, could have minimized the impact by rendering the exposed data unreadable to unauthorized parties.

Case Study 4: Anthem Healthcare Breach (2015)

- **Incident:** Attackers infiltrated Anthem Inc., exposing personal health information (PHI), including names, Social Security numbers, and medical data of nearly 80 million individuals.

- **Impact:** Anthem suffered major legal, financial, and reputational repercussions, including a record $115 million settlement and long-term compliance mandates.

- **Mitigation:** Encryption of PHI at rest, coupled with stricter access controls, would have minimized the breach's severity by making exposed data indecipherable and unusable by unauthorized parties.

Case Study 5: Yahoo data breach (2013–2014)

- **Incident:** Yahoo suffered a series of data breaches affecting billions of user accounts, compromising email addresses, passwords, and security questions.

- **Impact:** The breaches had severe consequences for Yahoo, including a significant decrease in company valuation and legal settlements.

- **Mitigation:** Strong encryption of stored passwords and security questions, along with regular security audits, could have mitigated the impact by protecting user data.

Cryptography in Practice Across Industries: Use-Case Scenarios and Business Value

The application of cryptography varies across sectors but remains universally critical. Whether securing online payments in e-commerce, protecting patient records in healthcare, or ensuring the integrity of classified government communications, cryptographic solutions are foundational to industry-specific security needs. This section showcases sectoral use cases—financial services, healthcare, telecommunications, e-commerce, and defense—illustrating how cryptography drives business value through trust, compliance, innovation, and risk mitigation. Business leaders can use these examples to benchmark their cryptographic readiness and align security investments with strategic outcomes.

Financial Services: Secure Transactions and Blockchain

Cryptography is at the core of secure financial transactions, ensuring the confidentiality and integrity of sensitive financial data. It also plays a crucial role in blockchain technology, providing a foundation for decentralized and tamper-proof ledgers [8].

Use cases in financial services:

- **Secure online banking:** Encryption protects online banking transactions, safeguarding customer information and preventing unauthorized access to accounts.

- **Digital payments:** Cryptography ensures the security of digital payment systems, such as credit cards and mobile payment apps, by encrypting transaction data.

- **Blockchain and cryptocurrencies:** Cryptographic techniques enable secure and transparent transactions in blockchain networks, supporting cryptocurrencies like Bitcoin and Ethereum.

- **Fraud detection and prevention:** Encryption and digital signatures enhance fraud detection and prevention by verifying the authenticity of transactions and user identities.

Business value:

- **Enhanced trust:** Strong encryption builds trust with customers by ensuring the security and privacy of their financial information.

- **Regulatory compliance:** Compliance with financial regulations, such as PCI DSS and GDPR, is facilitated through the use of encryption.

- **Innovation and efficiency:** Cryptographic solutions support innovation in financial services, enabling new business models and improving operational efficiency.

Healthcare: Protecting Patient Data

In the healthcare industry, cryptography plays a vital role in protecting patient data, ensuring privacy, and maintaining compliance with regulations like HIPAA [7].

Use cases in healthcare:

- **Electronic health records (EHRs):** Encryption safeguards patient information in EHRs, preventing unauthorized access and ensuring data confidentiality.

- **Telemedicine:** Secure encryption protocols protect patient–doctor communications during telemedicine consultations, ensuring privacy and data integrity.

- **Medical devices:** Cryptography ensures the security of medical devices connected to healthcare networks, preventing unauthorized access and tampering.

- **Data sharing:** Encryption facilitates secure data sharing between healthcare providers, ensuring that patient information is protected during transfers.

Business value:

- **Patient trust and privacy:** Encryption enhances patient trust by ensuring the confidentiality and security of their medical information.

- **Regulatory compliance:** Compliance with healthcare regulations, such as HIPAA, is supported by implementing encryption for data protection.

- **Improved patient care:** Secure access to patient data enables healthcare providers to deliver better patient care through accurate and timely information.

E-Commerce: Securing Customer Information

E-commerce businesses rely on cryptography to secure customer information, protect payment data, and ensure safe online shopping experiences [6, 8].

Use cases in e-commerce:

- **Secure payment processing:** Encryption protects payment card information during online transactions, ensuring the security of customer payment data.

- **Customer data protection:** Cryptography safeguards customer information, such as personal details and order history, preventing data breaches and identity theft.

- **Website security:** SSL/TLS encryption secures e-commerce websites, protecting customer interactions and transactions from eavesdropping and tampering.

- **Fraud prevention:** Encryption and digital signatures enhance fraud prevention by verifying the authenticity of transactions and user identities.

Business value:

- **Customer trust:** Strong encryption builds customer trust by ensuring the security of their personal and payment information during online shopping.

- **Regulatory compliance:** Compliance with data protection regulations, such as PCI DSS and GDPR, is facilitated through the use of encryption.

- **Competitive advantage:** Implementing robust cryptographic solutions enhances the reputation and competitiveness of e-commerce businesses.

Telecommunications: Ensuring Communication Privacy

In the telecommunications industry, cryptography ensures the privacy and security of communications, protecting sensitive information from unauthorized access and interception [1].

Use cases in telecommunications:

- **Secure voice and video calls:** Encryption protocols protect voice and video calls, ensuring that conversations remain private and secure.

- **Data transmission:** Cryptography safeguards data transmitted over telecommunications networks, preventing eavesdropping and data breaches.

- **Mobile security:** Encryption enhances the security of mobile devices and applications, protecting user data from unauthorized access.

- **Network security:** Cryptographic solutions secure telecommunications networks, preventing unauthorized access and ensuring data integrity.

Business value:

- **User privacy:** Encryption ensures the privacy and security of user communications, building trust and confidence in telecommunications services.

- **Regulatory compliance:** Compliance with telecommunications regulations and data protection standards is supported through the use of encryption.

- **Secure connectivity:** Cryptographic solutions enable secure connectivity and communication, enhancing the reliability and security of telecommunications networks.

Government and Defense: Classified Information Security

In government and defense sectors, cryptography is essential for protecting classified information, ensuring national security, and preventing unauthorized access to sensitive data [3].

Use cases in government and defense:

- **Secure communications:** Encryption protocols protect government communications, ensuring that sensitive information remains confidential and secure.

- **Classified data protection:** Cryptography safeguards classified data, preventing unauthorized access and protecting national security.

- **Identity verification:** Digital signatures and encryption enable secure identity verification for government personnel and contractors.

- **Cyber defense:** Cryptographic solutions enhance cyber defense capabilities, protecting government networks from cyber threats and attacks.

Business value:

- **National security:** Encryption ensures the confidentiality and security of sensitive government information, protecting national security interests.

- **Trust and reliability:** Implementing robust cryptographic solutions enhances the trust and reliability of government services and communications.

- **Cyber resilience:** Cryptography strengthens cyber resilience, protecting government networks and data from cyber threats and attacks.

Cryptography Technology and Solutions Architecture for Businesses

To derive maximum value from cryptography, organizations must integrate it into the broader context of enterprise IT architecture. This section outlines how to design and implement a cryptographic strategy that is aligned with business objectives and capable of withstanding current and emerging threats. From defining security policies to integrating encryption solutions and planning for quantum resilience, this section provides actionable guidance for building cryptographic architectures that are scalable, interoperable, and future-proof. It also introduces the tools and technologies available in the market, helping organizations evaluate and adopt the right solutions for their needs [4, 5].

Defining a Cryptographic Strategy

Defining a cryptographic strategy is essential for businesses to protect sensitive information, ensure compliance with regulations, and mitigate security risks. A well-defined cryptographic strategy encompasses key management, encryption policies, and risk assessments. There are seven key steps to define a cryptographic strategy as defined in the Figure 2-2.

Key steps in defining a cryptographic strategy:

- **Identify assets and risks:** Identify the assets that require protection, such as sensitive data, intellectual property, and customer information. Assess the risks associated with potential data breaches and security threats.

- **Define security objectives:** Establish clear security objectives that align with business goals, regulatory requirements, and industry standards.

- **Select cryptographic solutions:** Choose appropriate cryptographic solutions based on the identified assets, risks, and security objectives. Consider factors such as encryption algorithms, key lengths, and deployment models.

- **Implement key management:** Develop a robust key management strategy that encompasses key generation, distribution, storage, rotation, and revocation.

- **Establish encryption policies:** Define encryption policies and procedures that outline when and how encryption should be applied, ensuring consistent and effective implementation.

- **Conduct risk assessments:** Perform regular risk assessments to identify vulnerabilities and ensure that cryptographic solutions remain effective in addressing security threats.

- **Educate employees:** Train employees on cryptographic policies, best practices, and security awareness to minimize human errors and insider threats.

DEFINING A CRYPTOGRAPHIC STRATEGY

IDENTIFY ASSETS AND RISKS

DEFINE SECURITY OBJECTIVES

SELECT CRYPTOGRAPHIC SOLUTIONS

IMPLEMENT KEY MANAGEMENT

ESTABLISH ENCRYPTION POLICIES

CONDUCT RISK ASSESSMENTS

EDUCATE EMPLOYEES

Figure 2-2: Key steps in defining a cryptographic strategy

Integration of Cryptographic Solutions

Integrating cryptographic solutions into business processes and systems is crucial for achieving comprehensive data protection and security. Effective integration ensures that cryptography is seamlessly incorporated into existing workflows and technologies [4, 5].

Key considerations for integration:

- **Compatibility:** Ensure that cryptographic solutions are compatible with existing systems, applications, and infrastructure to avoid disruptions and inefficiencies.

- **Scalability:** Choose scalable cryptographic solutions that can accommodate business growth and evolving security requirements.

- **Performance:** Evaluate the performance impact of cryptographic solutions on systems and applications, ensuring that security measures do not compromise operational efficiency.

- **Interoperability:** Ensure that cryptographic solutions support interoperability with other security technologies and standards, facilitating seamless integration.

- **User experience:** Consider the user experience when integrating cryptographic solutions, ensuring that security measures do not impede usability or productivity.

Post-Quantum Cryptography

Emerging post-quantum cryptography (PQC) algorithms, are poised to revolutionize the field of cryptography, offering new approaches to secure communication and data protection.

Post-quantum cryptography algorithms are designed to withstand attacks from future cryptographically relevant quantum computers (CRQCs) as well as today's traditional computers [3].

Key features of post-quantum cryptography algorithms:

- **Quantum resistance:** Post-quantum cryptography algorithms provide security against quantum adversaries, ensuring that cryptographic systems remain secure in the quantum era.

- **Algorithm diversity:** Post-quantum cryptography encompasses a range of algorithmic approaches, including lattice-based, hash-based, isogeny-based, and multivariate quadratic equation-based cryptography.

Business implications:

- **Future-proof security:** Businesses adopting post-quantum cryptography algorithms can future-proof their security systems, mitigating the risks posed by quantum computing.

- **Research and development:** Investing in research and development of post-quantum cryptographic solutions positions businesses as leaders in innovation and security.

Tools and Software for Cryptographic Implementations

A variety of tools and software solutions are available for implementing cryptographic techniques in business environments. These tools facilitate encryption, key management, digital signatures, and secure communications.

Popular cryptographic tools and software:

- **OpenSSL:** OpenSSL is an open-source cryptographic library that provides a comprehensive suite of cryptographic functions.

- **GnuPG (GNU Privacy Guard):** GnuPG is an open-source tool for secure communication and data encryption, supporting a wide range of cryptographic algorithms.

- **HashiCorp Vault:** HashiCorp Vault is a tool for managing secrets, encryption keys, and access to sensitive data, providing robust security controls for key management.

- **Microsoft Azure Key Vault:** Azure Key Vault is a cloud-based service that enables secure storage and management of cryptographic keys, certificates, and secrets.

- **AWS Key Management Service (KMS):** AWS KMS is a managed service that allows businesses to create, control, and manage cryptographic keys for AWS applications.

Best Practices and Future Trends

Implementing cryptographic solutions requires adherence to best practices and awareness of emerging trends to ensure effective data protection and security.

Best practices for cryptographic implementations:

- **Use strong algorithms.** Select cryptographic algorithms recommended by industry standards, ensuring that they provide adequate security against modern threats.

- **Regularly update systems.** Keep cryptographic systems and software up-to-date to address vulnerabilities and enhance security features.

- **Conduct security audits.** Perform regular security audits and assessments to evaluate the effectiveness of cryptographic solutions and identify potential weaknesses.

- **Educate stakeholders.** Provide training and awareness programs for employees and stakeholders to promote a culture of security and ensure compliance with cryptographic policies.

- **Monitor emerging threats.** Stay informed about emerging threats and trends in cryptography, adapting security strategies as needed to address evolving risks.

Future trends in cryptography:

- **Quantum-safe cryptography (a.k.a. post-quantum cryptography or quantum-resistant cryptography):** As quantum computing advances, the development and adoption of cryptographic algorithms that are safe against both classical and quantum computer attacks.

- **Fully homomorphic encryption:** Fully homomorphic encryption, which allows computation on encrypted data without decryption, is gaining traction for secure data processing and analysis.

- **Zero-knowledge proofs:** Zero-knowledge proof is a cryptographic method that allows one party (called the prover) to prove to another party (the verifier) that a certain statement is true, without revealing any other information beyond the validity of the statement itself.

- **Blockchain and cryptography:** Cryptographic techniques will continue to play a crucial role in blockchain technology, supporting secure and transparent transactions in decentralized networks.

- **AI and cryptography:** The cryptographic solutions will be required to protect precious AI models from theft or loss.

Summary

Cryptography is a powerful and indispensable tool for businesses seeking to protect their data, ensure privacy, and maintain compliance in an increasingly digital world. By understanding the fundamental principles of cryptography, businesses can design and implement effective security strategies that mitigate risks and protect against cyber threats.

From secure communication to data protection and regulatory compliance, cryptography provides the foundation for building trust and resilience in business operations. As emerging technologies such as quantum computing and post-quantum cryptography continue to evolve, businesses must stay informed and adapt their security strategies to address new challenges and opportunities.

By adopting best practices, leveraging cutting-edge cryptographic solutions, and embracing a culture of security, businesses can navigate the complexities of the digital landscape with confidence and achieve lasting success in their security, privacy, and compliance endeavors [1, 3].

References

(1) IBM. (2025, May 28). *What Is Cryptography?* https://www.ibm.com/topics/cryptography.

(2) *Research | MIT CSAIL.* (n.d.). https://www.csail.mit.edu/research.

(3) NIST. (2025, June 18). NIST. https://www.nist.gov.

(4) *Key Vault | Microsoft Azure.* (n.d.). https://azure.microsoft.com/en-us/products/key-vault.

(5) AWS Key Management Service | Amazon. (n.d.). https://aws.amazon.com/kms.

(6) GDPR.eu. (2019, February 19). *General Data Protection Regulation (GDPR) Compliance Guidelines.* https://gdpr.eu.

(7) Department of Health & Human Services. (2025, June 19). *Health Insurance Portability and Accountability Act (HIPAA).* https://www.hhs.gov/hipaa/index.html.

(8) PCI Security Standards Council. (2025, June 16). *PCI Security Standards Council – Protect Payment Data with Industry-driven Security Standards, Training, and Programs.* https://www.pcisecuritystandards.org.

Understanding Classical and Post-Quantum Cryptography and Solutions

"Cryptography is an arms race between the designers of encryption algorithms and those who break them."

—Bruce Schneier

Cryptography is the bedrock of the security and safety of our digital world. Businesses depend on cryptography to safeguard critical assets and infrastructure against internal and external threats as well as to comply with security and privacy mandates. This includes protecting sensitive data, securing communications, authenticating digital identities, signing, and verifying electronic transactions. Individuals, perhaps without realizing it, also depend on cryptography to safeguard their personal information and their internet activities. This includes protecting personal data on their laptop computers, securing their online purchases and banking transactions, gaining access to their email and social media accounts, and digitally signing legal contracts. This chapter reviews classical cryptography and its applications, shows which subset thereof is vulnerable to attacks leveraging a cryptographically relevant quantum computer (CRQC), and outlines alternate algorithms that are safe against attacks originating from either classical or quantum computers.

Classical Cryptographic Algorithms and Their Applications

Chapter 2 provided a high-level introduction to classical cryptographic concepts and related technologies. Building on that introduction, we now explore these concepts in more detail and show how they are often combined in practice to build robust encryption solutions. As the industry globally prepares for the crucial transition to quantum-safe cryptography, this enhanced and practical understanding is paramount for both architects and technology executives to successfully drive this transition forward.

Symmetric, Asymmetric, and Hashing Algorithms

Symmetric algorithms are typically used for bulk data encryption because they are faster than asymmetric algorithms. For example, all major database, file system, object storage, tape, and disk encryption solutions use symmetric algorithms. As depicted in Figure 3-1, symmetric algorithms use the same key to encrypt and decrypt a given piece of data. The Advanced Encryption Standard (AES), Triple Data Encryption Standard (3DES), and Blowfish are some examples of widely known symmetric algorithms. Symmetric algorithms are generally characterized by their key sizes. The longer the key size, the stronger the security. For example, AES supports three key sizes: 128 bits, 192 bits, and 256 bits.

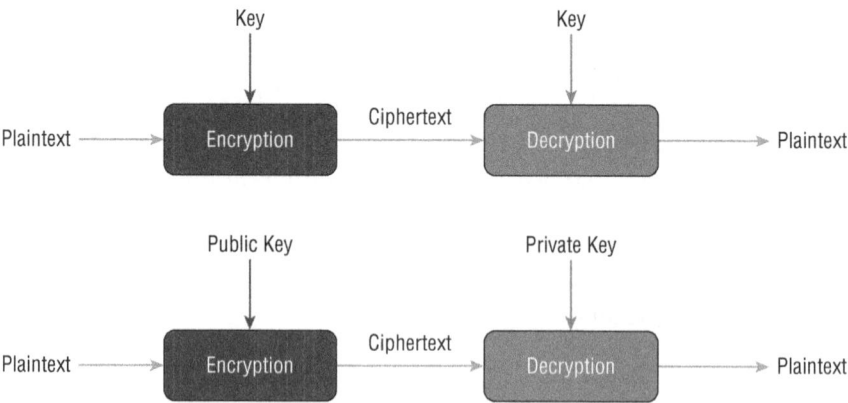

Figure 3-1: Symmetric algorithms vs. asymmetric algorithms

Asymmetric algorithms can also be used to encrypt data, but they are typically used for key exchange, digital signatures, and authentication. For example, in blockchain, an asymmetric algorithm is used to sign a transaction so that its authenticity can be verified. Unlike symmetric algorithms, asymmetric algorithms use two distinct keys, commonly referred to as the *private key* and *public key*. Data is encrypted using the public key and decrypted using the private key. Rivest-Shamir-Adleman (RSA), elliptic curve cryptography (ECC), and Diffie-Hellman (DH) are some examples of widely known asymmetric algorithms. Asymmetric algorithms are also generally characterized by their key sizes. The longer the key size, the stronger the security. For example, RSA is commonly used with 2048-bit or 4096-bit key sizes.

Hashing algorithms are typically used for message integrity, signature generation and verification, and password verification. For example, comparing message digests (hash digests over the message) calculated before and after transmission can determine whether any changes have been made to the message. Hashing algorithms apply a one-way function that takes as input a message of variable length and produces an output of a fixed length, called a message digest. SHA-256 and SHA-512 are examples of widely known hashing algorithms. Hashing algorithms are generally characterized by the size of their output (see Figure 3-2). The larger the size of the output, the stronger the security. For example, the output size of SHA-256 is 256 bits, and the output size of SHA-512 is 512 bits.

Original message → One-way hash function → Message digest

Figure 3-2: Hashing algorithms

Major Uses of Symmetric, Asymmetric, and Hashing Algorithms

Symmetric algorithms, asymmetric algorithms, and hashing algorithms are often combined to meet business objectives. For example, asymmetric algorithms and hashing algorithms are combined to create a *digital signature*. A digital signature is typically used to ensure both the authenticity and integrity of a document or message. First, a hashing algorithm is applied to the document or message to create a digest. The digest is then encrypted with an asymmetric algorithm using the private key. The output produced is called a *signature*. On the receiving side, the signature is decrypted using the public key. The resulting digest is compared with the digest computed by the receiver after applying the same hashing algorithm on the received document or message. If the two digests match, the signature is verified. Figure 3-3 summarizes the digital signature and verification process.

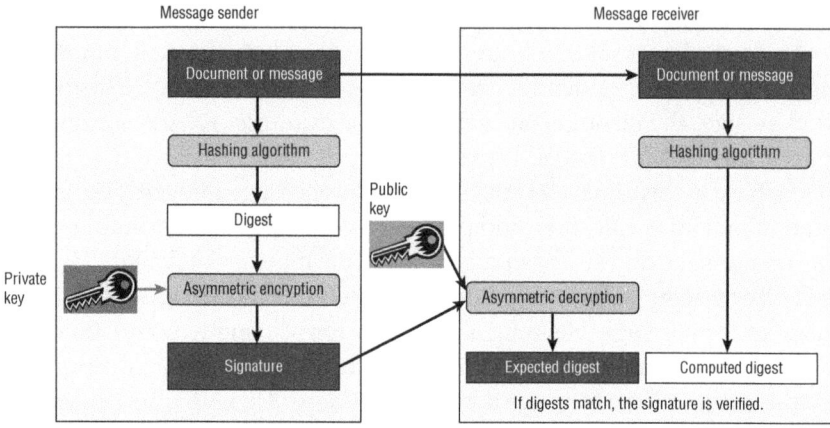

Figure 3-3: The digital signature and verification process

Digital signatures are also used in the creation of *digital certificates*. A digital certificate is typically used to prove the authenticity of a user, device, or application. Upon confirmation of the identity of the user, device, or application, a *certificate authority* (CA) signs the digital certificate and issues it to them so they can use it to prove their identity to other systems.

Table 3-1 summarizes the major classical cryptographic algorithms and their use.

Table 3-1: Major Uses of Symmetric, Asymmetric, and Hashing Algorithms

CRYPTOGRAPHIC ALGORITHM	ENCRYPTION	HASHING	DIGITAL SIGNATURE	KEY EXCHANGE
Rivest-Shamir-Adleman (RSA)	✓		✓	✓
Elliptic Curve Cryptography (ECC)	✓		✓	✓

CRYPTOGRAPHIC ALGORITHM	ENCRYPTION	HASHING	DIGITAL SIGNATURE	KEY EXCHANGE
Digital Signature Algorithm (DSA)			✓	
Advanced Encryption Standard (AES)	✓			
Triple Data Encryption Standard (3DES)	✓			
Blowfish	✓			
SHA-256, SHA-512		✓		

Real-World Applications of Classical Cryptography

Symmetric algorithms, asymmetric algorithms, hashing algorithms, digital signatures, digital certificates, and CAs are the building blocks on which solutions to real-world security problems are built. In this section, we describe three key examples where these building blocks are put to work: code signing, secure communication, and data-at-rest encryption.

Code signing is a critical requirement to ensure the authenticity and integrity of software as well as to limit the propagation of malware. The code signing process brings together a digital certificate, a CA, and a digital signature. The digital certificate includes the identity and public key of the software publisher as well as the signature of the CA that validated such identity. To sign the code, the process typically goes as follows:

1. The publisher applies a hashing algorithm to the original code, producing a digest.

2. The publisher signs the digest produced with their private key, producing a digital signature.

3. The publisher adds the digital signature and their digital certificate to the original code, producing a signed code package.

The signed code package can then safely be shared with consumers. To verify that the signed code package has not been tampered with and is from a trusted publisher, the process typically goes as follows:

1. The consumer decrypts the digital signature using the included digital certificate, producing the original digest.

2. The consumer applies the same hashing algorithm as the publisher to the code received, producing a new digest.

3. The consumer compares both digests. If they match, this proves that the code has not been tampered with.

4. The consumer verifies the authenticity of the publisher's digital certificate included in the signed code package. If the authenticity is verified and the code has not been tampered with, then the code can be safely consumed.

Secure communication is a critical requirement to ensure the confidentiality and integrity of data in transit. Examples of secure communication protocols include Transport Layer Security (TLS), Hypertext Transfer Protocol Secure (HTTPS), and Internet Protocol Security (IPsec).

Although the implementation details may differ, the secure communication process typically brings together symmetric algorithms, asymmetric algorithms, hashing algorithms, and digital certificates. An asymmetric algorithm is used in the protocol handshake phase to agree on a symmetric key (key exchange), and then a symmetric algorithm is used to encrypt the actual data communication using that symmetric key. A hashing algorithm is also used in this context to ensure the integrity of the messages exchanged between the sender and receiver. Additionally, digital certificates may be used so that the two parties involved in the communication can mutually authenticate each other.

Data-at-rest encryption is a critical requirement to ensure the confidentiality of critical data and is typically required to comply with data security compliance mandates such as the European General Data Protection Regulation (GDPR), the U.S. Health Insurance Portability and Accountability Act (HIPAA), and the Payment Card Industry Data Security Standard (PCI DSS). Data-at-rest encryption comes in many shapes and forms, ranging from self-encrypting disks, to file system encryption, to database encryption, all the way to column and field level encryption [1].

Although the implementation details may differ, the data-at-rest encryption process typically brings together a symmetric algorithm, a data encryption key (DEK), and a master key (MK). The symmetric algorithm is usually AES. The DEK is used to encrypt the actual data and is typically stored (encrypted) in the data system itself. For example, in the IBM DB2 Transparent Data Encryption implementation [1], the DEK is used to encrypt database objects such as tables, indexes, and transaction logs and is stored in the database. The MK is a key encryption key (KEK) and is used to encrypt the DEK. The MK is typically stored outside the database, such as in a hardware security module (HSM). Figure 3-4 depicts the IBM DB2 database encryption architecture.

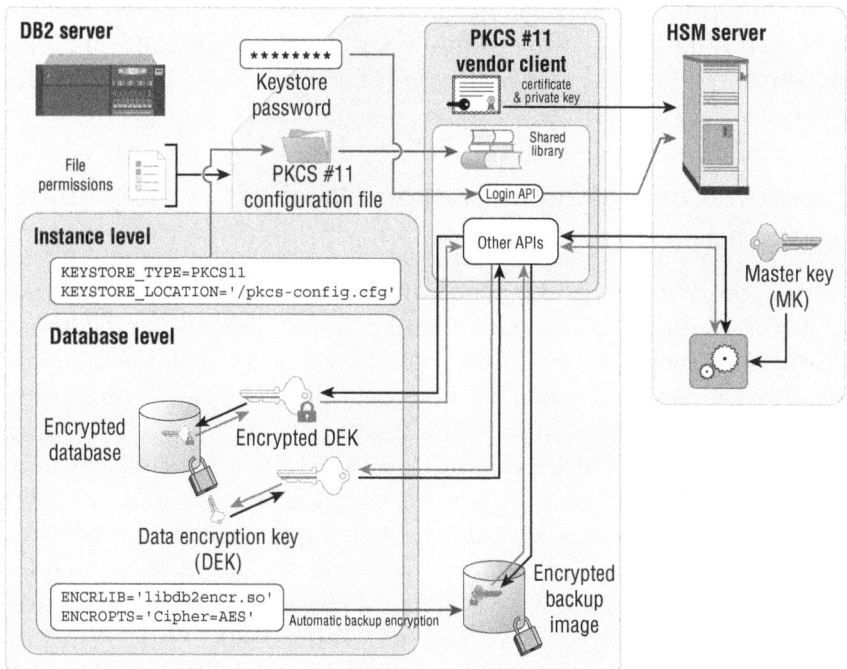

Figure 3-4: The IBM DB2 database encryption architecture

Post-Quantum Cryptography

With the vast increase in computing power, quantum computers promise to revolutionize many fields, including artificial intelligence, medicine, and space exploration. But they may also be abused to break key cryptographic algorithms we depend upon for the safety of our digital world. This poses a risk for a wide range of areas, such as securing data communications, signing certificates for establishing trust, signing financial transactions in blockchain, signing software for secure distribution, signing legal documents, verifying the authenticity of messages, and protecting sensitive data. Fortunately, alternate cryptographic algorithms that are safe against attacks by both quantum and classical computers do exist. These alternatives are commonly referred to as post-quantum cryptography (PQC) algorithms. The US National Institute of Standards and Technology (NIST) has already standardized a subset of such alternatives back in August 2024 [2]. In total, three PQC algorithms have been standardized by NIST: one for key encapsulation (Module-Lattice-Based Key-Encapsulation Mechanism [ML-KEM]) and two for digital signature (Module-Lattice-Based Digital Signature Algorithm [ML-DSA] and Stateless Hash-Based Digital Signature Algorithm [SLH-DSA]).

Quantum Computing Impact on Classical Cryptographic Algorithms

It is essential to understand that quantum computing will affect classical cryptography differently depending on the class of classical cryptographic algorithms. Asymmetric algorithms based on factoring large integers (e.g., RSA) and those based on discrete logarithms (e.g., DH) will simply need to be replaced by quantum-safe alternatives such as ML-KEM and ML-DSA. Effective security strength, shown in Table 3-2, suggests that the strength of RSA and ECC is somewhat weaker or comparable to AES on a classical computer but is null on a quantum computer. This is because Shor's algorithm [3] can perform integer factorization in polynomial time. In other words, what requires millions of years with classical computers would take only hours on a CRQC.

Unlike asymmetric algorithms, symmetric algorithms do not face an existential threat. However, a quantum computer running Grover's algorithm [4] could provide a quadratic improvement in brute-force attacks on symmetric algorithms such as AES. This translates into a need to double the key size to support the same level of protection. For AES specifically, this means using 256-bit keys to maintain today's 128-bit security strength, as depicted in Table 3-2. Hashing algorithms are similarly affected by Grover's algorithm. For example, although SHA-256 is still considered secure against classical attacks, it is only as secure as a 128-bit hash against quantum attacks.

Table 3-2: The Effective Security Strength of Key Classical Algorithms

CLASSICAL CRYPTOGRAPHIC ALGORITHM EXAMPLE	KEY/HASH SIZE (BITS)	EFFECTIVE SECURITY ON CLASSICAL COMPUTERS (BITS)	EFFECTIVE SECURITY ON QUANTUM COMPUTERS (BITS)
RSA-1024	1024	80	0
RSA-2048	2048	112	0
ECC-256	256	128	0
ECC-384	384	256	0
AES-128	128	128	64
AES-256	256	256	128
SHA-256	256	256	128
SHA-512	512	512	256

Post-Quantum Cryptographic Algorithms

Post-quantum cryptography (PQC) refers to a set of cryptographic algorithms that run on classical computers and are safe against attacks by both classical and quantum computers. The best-known examples of PQC algorithms are those that have been standardized by NIST: ML-KEM, ML-DSA, and SLH-DSA [2].

ML-KEM, formerly known as CRYSTALS-Kyber, is a key encapsulation mechanism (KEM) whose security is based on the difficulty of solving the learning-with-errors (LWE) problem over module lattices [5]. ML-KEM is a quantum-safe algorithm and is a member of the CRYSTALS (Cryptographic Suite for Algebraic Lattices) suite of algorithms. Federal Information Processing Standards (FIPS) 203 is the NIST standard that specifies the ML-KEM algorithm.

Variants of the algorithm with different security levels have been defined (see Table 3-3). More specifically, ML-KEM-512 targets security roughly equivalent to that of AES-128, ML-KEM-768 targets security roughly equivalent to that of AES-192, and ML-KEM-1024 targets security roughly equivalent to that of AES-256. These security levels have different characteristics when it comes to key and ciphertext sizes. For example, at the ML-KEM-512 level, the private keys are 1632 bytes in size, the public keys 800 bytes, and the ciphertexts 768 bytes. At the ML-KEM-768 level, the private keys are 2400 bytes in size, the public keys 1184 bytes, and the ciphertexts 1088 bytes. At the ML-KEM-1024 level, the private keys are 3168 bytes in size, the public keys 1568 bytes, and the ciphertexts 1568 bytes.

Table 3-3: ML-KEM Key and Ciphertext Sizes for Different Security Levels

PARAMETER SET	NIST SECURITY LEVEL	PRIVATE KEY SIZE (BYTES)	PUBLIC KEY SIZE (BYTES)	CIPHERTEXT SIZE (BYTES)
ML-KEM-512	1 (AES-128)	1632	800	768
ML-KEM-768	3 (AES-192)	2400	1184	1088
ML-KEM-1024	5 (AES-256)	3168	1568	1568

ML-KEM can be used as a quantum-safe alternative to classical algorithms such as RSA and DH. It can also be used in combination with such algorithms in what is referred to as *hybrid mode*. Examples of hybrid mode implementations involving ML-KEM include the AWS Key Management Service [6], IBM Z16 [7], and IBM DB2 [8].

ML-DSA, formerly known as CRYSTALS-Dilithium, is a lattice-based signature algorithm based on the LWE module and short integer solution (SIS) module problems [9]. The ML-DSA signature algorithm is a quantum-safe algorithm and is a member of the CRYSTALS suite of algorithms. FIPS 204 is the NIST standard that specifies the ML-DSA algorithm.

The construction of ML-DSA follows the Fiat–Shamir with aborts paradigm that was invented by IBM Researcher Vadim Lyubashevsky [9]. Variants of the algorithm with different security levels have been defined (see Table 3-4). More specifically, ML-DSA-44 targets security roughly equivalent to that of AES-128, ML-DSA-65 targets security roughly equivalent to that of AES-192, and ML-DSA-87 targets security roughly equivalent to that of AES-256. These security levels have different characteristics when it comes to key and signature sizes. For example, with ML-DSA-44, the signature size is 2420 bytes. The combined key and signature size of ML-DSA is the smallest of the two signature algorithms that have been standardized by NIST.

ML-DSA can be used as a quantum-safe alternative to classical algorithms such as RSA, ECC, and DSA. It can also be used in combination

Table 3-4: ML-DSA Key and Signature Sizes for Different Security Levels

PARAMETER SET	NIST SECURITY LEVEL	PRIVATE KEY SIZE (BYTES)	PUBLIC KEY SIZE (BYTES)	SIGNATURE SIZE (BYTES)
ML-DSA-44	1 (AES-128)	2560	1312	2420
ML-DSA-65	3 (AES-192)	4032	1952	1088
ML-DSA-87	5 (AES-256)	4896	2592	1568

with such algorithms when a hybrid mode implementation is desired. Examples of hybrid mode implementations involving ML-DSA include IBM Z16 [7] and IBM DB2 [8].

SLH-DSA, formerly known as SPHINCS⁺, is also a quantum-safe digital signature algorithm, but unlike ML-DSA, it is not based on lattices. Instead, SLH-DSA is a stateless hash-based signature algorithm. It can be instantiated using one of two hash functions: SHAKE and SHA2. FIPS 205 is the NIST standard that specifies the SLH-DSA algorithm.

Variants of the algorithm with different security levels have been defined (see Table 3-5). More specifically, SLH-DSA-SHA2-128s and SLH-DSA-SHAKE-128s target security roughly equivalent to that of AES-128, SLH-DSA-SHA2-192s and SLH-DSA-SHAKE-192s target security roughly equivalent to that of AES-192, and SLH-DSA-SHA2-256s and SLH-DSA-SHAKE-256s target security roughly equivalent to that of AES-256. These security levels have different characteristics when it comes to key and ciphertext sizes. For example, with DSA-SHA2-128s, the signature size is 7856 bytes. The combined key and signature size of SLH-DSA is the largest among the two signature algorithms that have been standardized by NIST.

Table 3-5: SLH-DSA Key and Signature Sizes for Different Security Levels

PARAMETER SET	NIST SECURITY LEVEL	PUBLIC KEY SIZE (BYTES)	SIGNATURE SIZE (BYTES)
SLH-DSA-SHA2-128s	1 (AES-128)	32	7856
SLH-DSA-SHAKE-128s			
SLH-DSA-SHA2-128f	1 (AES-128)	32	17088
SLH-DSA-SHAKE-128f			

Continues

Table 3-5 *(continued)*

PARAMETER SET	NIST SECURITY LEVEL	PUBLIC KEY SIZE (BYTES)	SIGNATURE SIZE (BYTES)
SLH-DSA-SHA2-192s	3 (AES-192)	48	16224
SLH-DSA-SHAKE-192s			
SLH-DSA-SHA2-192f	3 (AES-192)	48	35664
SLH-DSA-SHAKE-192f			
SLH-DSA-SHA2-256s	5 (AES-256)	64	29792
SLH-DSA-SHAKE-256s			
SLH-DSA-SHA2-256f	5 (AES-256)	64	49856
SLH-DSA-SHAKE-256f			

SLH-DSA can be used as a quantum-safe alternative to classical algorithms such as RSA, ECC, and DSA. It can also be used in combination with such algorithms when a hybrid mode implementation is desired. An example of a hybrid mode implementation involving SLH-DSA is the Thales Luna HSM [10].

Additional Quantum-Safe Technologies

Besides PQC, other quantum-safe technologies have been introduced to help counter the security risks posed by quantum computing. The most widely known examples of such technologies are quantum key distribution (QKD) and quantum random number generators (QRNGs).

Quantum Key Distribution

The security of the PQC algorithms discussed earlier is based on hard mathematical problems. On the other hand, the security of QKD is based on fundamental properties of quantum physics. That is, the mere act of measuring a quantum system disturbs that system, and consequently, any eavesdropper trying to intercept a quantum exchange will inevitably be detected. A QKD protocol implementation typically includes the following aspects:

▪ A fiber-optic quantum communication channel to send quantum states of light (photons) between a sender (Alice) and a receiver (Bob). This channel does not need to be secured.

▪ A classic communication channel between the two parties to perform post-processing steps and derive a shared secret key. This channel must be authenticated.

The most famous QKD protocol is BB84, which is named after its inventors: Charles Bennett of IBM and Gilles Brassard of the University of Montreal [11]. The sender (Alice) and receiver (Bob) typically implement this protocol by exchanging single photons over a fiber-optic channel, whose polarization states are used to encode bit values. ID Quantique QKD is one example of a commercial system that implements the BB84 protocol. QKD does not actually require a quantum computer, but it uses quantum effects such as photons in the key distribution process.

QKD has the key advantage that its security is not threatened by computing power or advancement in mathematics. Its security stems from quantum physics properties, as discussed previously. On the other hand, QKD is more intrusive to an organization's IT infrastructure than the PQC algorithms, as it requires injecting new devices to leverage quantum physics for key distribution.

Quantum Random Number Generators

Random number generation is essential in cryptography. Classical random generation methods can be divided into two main categories: pseudo random number generators (PRNGs) and true random number generators (TRNGs). A PRNG produces random numbers from a deterministic algorithm. Clearly, any algorithmically generated sequence cannot be truly random. Therefore, this method is not typically suitable for generating strong encryption keys. On the other hand, a TRNG measures some unpredictable physical process and uses the results to create random numbers. Some of the typical entropy sources this process uses include data from disk access times, timing of interrupts, and user interaction data such as mouse motion or keystrokes. There are also physical TRNGs based on principles such as thermal noise in electronic circuits. The TRNG on the Intel Ivy Bridge processors is one such example. Clearly, TRNGs are more suitable for generating strong encryption keys.

QRNGs can be thought of as a special case of TRNGs in which the data is the result of quantum events. But unlike classical TRNGs, QRNGs promise truly random numbers by exploiting the inherent randomness in quantum physics. Some examples of QRNG implementations include QUANTIS from ID Quantique and Luna HSM from Thales [10]. QRNGs do not actually require a quantum computer, but they use quantum effects such as photons in the process of generating random numbers.

Contrasting Quantum-Safe Technologies

As organizations prepare to transition to quantum-safe cryptographic implementations, it is critical to understand what specific problems each quantum-safe technology addresses. Organizations typically implement cryptography to achieve four key objectives:

- **Confidentiality:** This is the use case where data is encrypted, such as when it is at rest, in transit, or in use. Symmetric algorithms such as AES are typically used to achieve this objective.

- **Integrity:** This is the use case where safeguards need to be put in place to protect against malicious or accidental changes to data. Hashing and signing algorithms are typically used to achieve this objective.

- **Authentication:** This is the use case where users or devices must be authenticated before they are granted access to data, systems, or applications. Asymmetric algorithms are typically used to achieve this objective.

- **Nonrepudiation:** This is the use case where individuals must be held accountable for their actions, such as a document they signed or an email they sent. Signing algorithms are typically used to achieve this objective.

Table 3-6 contrasts quantum-safe technologies with respect to confidentiality, integrity, authentication, and nonrepudiation.

Table 3-6: Contrasting Quantum-Safe Technologies

QUANTUM-SAFE TECHNOLOGY	CONFIDEN-TIALITY	INTEGRITY	AUTHENTI-CATION	NONREPU-DIATION
Post-quantum cryptography (PQC)	✓	✓	✓	✓
Quantum key distribution (QKD)	✓	X	X	X
Quantum random number generator (QRNG)	X	X	X	X

As Table 3-6 clearly shows, PQC will be critical for any organization to transition to quantum-safe cryptographic implementations. Additionally, PQC is a natural evolution from classical cryptography as it does not require the injection of any new IT infrastructure components as QKD does. QRNGs do not necessarily require the injection of new IT infrastructure because they are being included in existing HSMs such as the Luna HSM from Thales [10]. They contribute to producing high-quality entropy, which is the basis for all random numbers and cryptographic keys generated by any HSM.

Summary

This chapter provided a comprehensive overview of both classical and post-quantum cryptographic algorithms, emphasizing their role in securing our digital world. It began by detailing classical cryptographic algorithms and how they are often combined in real-world applications such as code signing, secure communication, and data-at-rest encryption. The chapter then explored the looming threat posed by quantum computers, particularly their ability to break widely used asymmetric cryptography via Shor's algorithm while also weakening symmetric cryptography and hashing through Grover's algorithm. Next, we introduced quantum-safe alternatives standardized by NIST—ML-KEM, ML-DSA, and SLH-DSA—detailing their structure, use cases, and security levels. Finally, the chapter contrasted post-quantum cryptography with other quantum-safe technologies such as quantum key distribution (QKD) and quantum random number generators (QRNGs), highlighting their distinct roles and deployment implications.

References

(1) W. Rjaibi, "Holistic Database Encryption," in *Proceedings of the Fifteenth International Conference on Security and Cryptography (SECRYPT)*, Porto, Portugal, 2018.

(2) US NIST, "Post Quantum Cryptography," https://csrc.nist .gov/Projects/post-quantum-cryptography.

(3) P. Shor, "Polynomial time algorithms for prime factorization and discrete logarithms on a quantum," *SIAM Journal on Computing*, 26(5), 1484–1509.

(4) L. Grover, "A fast quantum mechanical algorithm for database search," in *Proceedings of the Twenty-Eighth Annual ACM Symposium on Theory of Computing*, 1996.

(5) J. Bos, L. Ducas, E. Kiltz, T. Lepoint, V. Lyubashevsky, J. Schanck, P. Schwabe, G. Seiler, D. Stehlé, "CRYSTALS – Kyber: a CCA-secure module-lattice-based KEM," in *IEEE European Symposium on Security and Privacy (EuroS&P)*, 2018.

(6) AWS Key Management Service (KMS) Online Product Documentation, `https://docs.aws.amazon.com/kms/latest/developerguide/pqtls.html`.

(7) IBM Z16 Online Product Documentation, `https://research.ibm.com/blog/z16-quantum-safe-migration`.

(8) L. Zhang, A. Miranskyy, W. Rjaibi, G. Stager, M. Gray, J. Peck, J., "Making Existing Software Quantum Safe: A Case Study on IBM DB2," in *ELSEVIER Information and Software Technology Journal*, 2023.

(9) J. Bos, L. Ducas, E. Kiltz, T. Lepoint, V. Lyubashevsky, J. Schanck, P. Schwabe, G. Seiler, D. Stehlé, "CRYSTALS-Dilithium – Algorithm Specifications and Supporting Documentation," `https://pq-crystals.org/dilithium/data/dilithium-specification-round3-20210208.pdf`.

(10) Thales Online Product Documentation, `https://www.thalestct.com/luna-network-hsm`.

(11) US NSA, "Quantum Key Distribution (QKD) and Quantum Cryptography (QC)," `https://www.nsa.gov/Cybersecurity/Quantum-Key-Distribution-QKD-and-Quantum-Cryptography-QC`.

Managing Risks in the Quantum Era

"There is no security without uncertainty, and no progress without risk."

—Niels Bohr

The advent of quantum computing brings a transformative era of technological advancement, promising breakthroughs in various fields. However, it also introduces significant cybersecurity risks. Quantum computers, with their unparalleled processing power, can potentially break the cryptographic algorithms that currently secure digital communications and data. This chapter delves into the intricacies of managing cyber risks in the post-quantum era, providing a comprehensive framework for identifying, assessing, mitigating, and monitoring these new threats [1].

Identifying Quantum-Related Business Risks and Impacts

Quantum computing is advancing at a pace that challenges long-standing assumptions about the durability of digital security. As quantum processors gain the capability to solve problems that underpin modern cryptographic systems, businesses are entering a new risk era. The first step in responding effectively is to identify quantum-related threats with precision—and then assess their potential impact across the enterprise.

This section outlines two essential parts of quantum risk awareness: the identification of specific risks and the analysis of how those risks translate into tangible business impacts. Through this structure, business and technology leaders can better align mitigation strategies with their organizational priorities.

Identifying Quantum Risk

Quantum computing introduces new risks primarily by weakening or defeating classical cryptographic techniques. The ability to factor large numbers and search large key spaces efficiently puts current public-key infrastructure (PKI) and symmetric encryption at risk.

To identify these risks effectively, organizations must conduct a detailed analysis of where and how cryptography is deployed. This involves asset discovery, algorithm classification, and evaluation of exposure. Following are the primary risk areas to consider.

Cryptographic Vulnerabilities

Organizations must assess the types of cryptographic algorithms used across their systems. Public-key systems such as RSA, ECC, and DH are particularly vulnerable to Shor's algorithm. Symmetric systems like AES are less vulnerable, but Grover's algorithm reduces their effective key strength. The risk identification steps are as follows:

- Conduct an enterprise-wide cryptographic inventory.
- Discover all uses of RSA, ECC, DH, and outdated symmetric ciphers.
- Scan applications, APIs, databases, and network communications for cryptographic endpoints.

Data Classification and Sensitivity

Not all data is equally at risk. Data that is highly sensitive or requires long-term protection is particularly vulnerable to "harvest now and decrypt later" (HNDL) attacks. Here are the steps to identify risks:

- Classify data based on sensitivity and retention requirements.

- Map data types (e.g., PII, PHI, financial records, contracts) to their encryption methods.

- Evaluate external-facing applications and services for encryption strength.

Authentication and Identity Systems

Digital signatures and identity verification mechanisms often rely on public-key cryptography. Quantum computing could compromise authentication protocols, enabling impersonation attacks. Follow these steps:

- Review authentication protocols (e.g., PKI, SAML, TLS, SSH) in internal and external services.

- Identify dependencies on digital signatures for code validation and document integrity.

- Audit systems for hardcoded or expired credentials.

Supply Chain Dependencies

Quantum risks extend beyond the enterprise to third-party vendors and suppliers. Software updates, signed binaries, and cloud APIs all depend on trusted encryption. Follow these risk-identification steps:

- Conduct software bill of materials (SBOM) and cryptography BOM (CBOM) scans.

- Assess supplier encryption practices and post-quantum cryptography (PQC) readiness.

- Audit digital signature verification in code and firmware updates.

Regulatory Exposure

Regulators are beginning to mandate quantum preparedness. Organizations that fail to identify cryptographic risks will likely fall out of compliance with emerging standards. Here are the steps to identify risks:

- Compare your cryptographic inventory against NIST, NSA, CNSA 2.0, and ENISA recommendations.

- Review audit logs and governance policies for cryptographic decision-making.

- Engage compliance teams to prepare for future PQC regulations [3].

Evaluating the Business Impacts of Quantum Risks

Once quantum risks are identified, the next step is to assess their potential impact on business operations, customer trust, financial stability, and regulatory compliance. The following categories illustrate how quantum threats manifest as tangible business consequences.

Data Breaches and Financial Losses

Compromised encryption can lead to unauthorized access to sensitive data, resulting in regulatory penalties, customer compensation, and long-term reputational damage. In sectors like banking and healthcare, the financial implications can be catastrophic. Here are some examples of business impact:

- Breach of encrypted customer financial records
- Lawsuits due to GDPR or HIPAA violations
- Stock price decline following public disclosure [7]

Intellectual Property Theft

Companies that rely on innovation may face exposure of their trade secrets if R&D communications are intercepted and decrypted post facto. This could result in a loss of competitive advantage or undermine strategic partnerships. These are examples of business impact:

- Theft of product designs or drug formulas
- Premature exposure of patentable innovations
- Strategic espionage from nation-state actors

Operational Disruption

Authentication failures and certificate compromises could interrupt core business functions. In sectors such as transportation, manufacturing, or energy, this could lead to halted operations and public safety risks. Here are some examples of business impact:

- Outages in smart grid or Supervisory Control and Data Acquisition (SCADA) systems
- System-wide denial of service due to broken TLS trust chains
- Suspension of cloud-based productivity platforms

Supply Chain Breakdown

When cryptographic trust is broken in a supply chain, malicious code or counterfeit products can enter operational environments undetected. Organizations may suffer from delayed services, security breaches, or customer dissatisfaction. These are some examples of business impact:

- Tampered software updates from compromised vendors
- Loss of trust in the vendor ecosystem
- Regulatory liability for downstream product failures

Regulatory and Contractual Noncompliance

Organizations may face penalties, contract termination, or exclusion from procurement processes if they do not meet evolving cryptographic standards. Here are some examples of business impact:

- Ineligibility for defense or government contracts
- Fines for lack of quantum-safe controls
- Negative audit results impacting investor confidence

Quantum computing introduces a spectrum of risks that extend across data confidentiality, system integrity, and regulatory compliance. To mitigate these threats, organizations must first identify where quantum vulnerabilities exist—from encryption protocols and authentication systems to vendor integrations and data repositories.

Following identification, it is essential to assess the business impact of these risks. Only with a dual focus on discovery and consequences can leaders prioritize remediation efforts, allocate resources wisely, and build resilient, quantum-safe infrastructures.

By treating quantum risk as both a technical and a strategic imperative, organizations can shift from passive observers to proactive innovators in a post-quantum world.

Building a Robust Risk Management Framework Against Quantum Threats

Organizations must adopt a strategic approach to mitigate against quantum threats by building a robust risk management framework tailored to the quantum era.

Creating a robust structure and implementing such a framework will provide practical guidance to business and technical leaders. The process focuses on five core pillars: governance, discovery, risk classification, crypto-agility, and continuous monitoring. The following sections include detailed narratives and supporting visuals to equip decision-makers with the understanding required to initiate and sustain a post-quantum transformation.

Establishing Foundational Principles

Before delving into building the risk management framework (see Figure 4-1), it is essential to ground the framework in guiding principles that ensure both effectiveness and sustainability. Proactivity is key: organizations must prepare for quantum threats well before they materialize. The framework must be comprehensive, spanning the entire digital estate, including third-party vendors and embedded devices. Flexibility is equally vital, allowing for changes in cryptographic standards, regulatory requirements, and threat intelligence. Finally, the framework should be measurable, with well-defined key performance indicators (KPIs), risk scores, and audit trails.

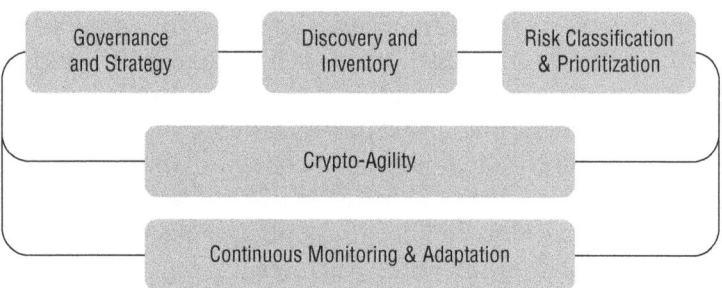

Figure 4-1: Quantum risk management framework

Governance and Strategic Oversight

Effective governance begins with executive recognition of the quantum threat. Organizations should establish a Quantum Risk Council that operates as a central body for strategy, funding, and cross-functional alignment. This council must include stakeholders from cybersecurity, IT operations, legal, compliance, product development, and risk management. Together, they define post-quantum security objectives, align them with enterprise risk management (ERM), and integrate quantum considerations into organizational strategy.

The role of the council extends to setting organizational priorities, allocating resources, and tracking readiness. Governance also requires strong internal communication and ongoing education to ensure buy-in at all levels. By embedding quantum risk awareness into boardroom discussions, organizations elevate the issue from a technical concern to a strategic imperative.

Cryptographic Discovery and Inventory

One of the most challenging aspects of quantum risk management is achieving full visibility into the use of cryptography across an enterprise. Most organizations use encryption in far more places than they realize—from TLS and SSH in web servers to embedded encryption in firmware, APIs, third-party platforms, and even continuous integration and continuous delivery (CICD) pipelines. Without knowing where cryptography exists, it is impossible to protect it.

Organizations must begin by deploying discovery tools designed to scan systems, applications, databases, and network traffic. These tools generate a CBOM that details the algorithms, key lengths, certificates, and cryptographic libraries in use. Categorizing this data by use case—such as data-at-rest encryption, digital signatures, or key exchanges—enables a comprehensive understanding of cryptographic dependencies. Figure 4-2 shows the cryptographic discovery & inventory process [2].

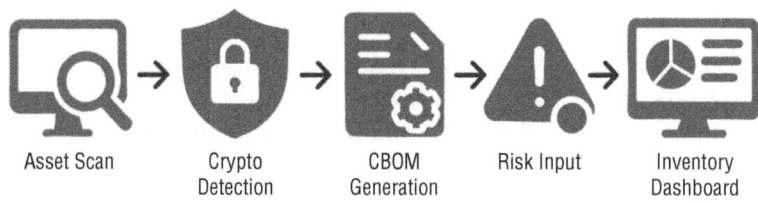

| Asset Scan | Crypto Detection | CBOM Generation | Risk Input | Inventory Dashboard |

Figure 4-2: Cryptographic discovery and inventory process

Risk Classification and Prioritization

Identifying cryptographic assets is only the beginning. The next step involves assessing their risk in the context of quantum threats.

Classification helps organizations determine which assets require urgent remediation and which can be addressed over time [5].

Risk classification is based on several dimensions: the sensitivity of the data being protected, the exposure level of the system (e.g., internet-facing versus internal-only), and the impact that cryptographic failure would have on business operations. Assets can be plotted on a heat map to visualize their criticality.

Enabling Crypto-Agility

Crypto-agility is the enterprise's ability to swiftly and securely adapt cryptographic mechanisms: updating algorithms when broken, changing them in response to regulatory mandates, monitoring their use across environments, and retiring them when obsolete. Achieving crypto-agility requires more than reactive patchwork. It demands a framework-led strategy that is proactive, scalable, and continuous [6]. This framework is founded on five core principles:

1. **Architectural modularity and abstraction:** Design systems to separate cryptographic logic from business logic, enabling seamless cryptographic updates without rewriting applications. Abstraction layers allow swapping of algorithms without disrupting workflows.

2. **Automation and orchestration:** Leverage dynamic cryptographic discovery, enterprise-wide CBOMs, key lifecycle automation, and continuous compliance checks. Automation reduces human error, accelerates response to vulnerabilities, and ensures cryptographic hygiene across DevSecOps pipelines.

3. **Governance and policy enforcement:** Establish clear policies for cryptographic use, centrally manage crypto-inventories using CBOMs, enforce algorithm usage standards, and ensure traceable auditing. Supply chain cryptographic risk must be embedded in governance, risk, and compliance oversight.

4. **Continuous monitoring and posture management:** Implement real-time analytics and cryptographic telemetry to track usage, validate configurations, and detect misapplications or drifts from policy.

5. **Interoperability and ecosystem agility:** Enable crypto-agility across multi-cloud, hybrid, and third-party ecosystems by enforcing standards-based cryptographic interfaces, promoting vendor-neutral solutions, and integrating secure cryptographic agility protocols.

Crypto-agility is not simply a security enhancement—it's a business imperative. The organizations that succeed in enabling crypto-agility will be those that can respond to threats more quickly, meet compliance demands confidently, and preserve digital trust in the face of inevitable cryptographic change. The five-principle framework, as shown in Figure 4-3, empowers leaders to transform reactive, fragmented cryptographic practices into a proactive, enterprise-wide capability for resilience and competitive advantage.

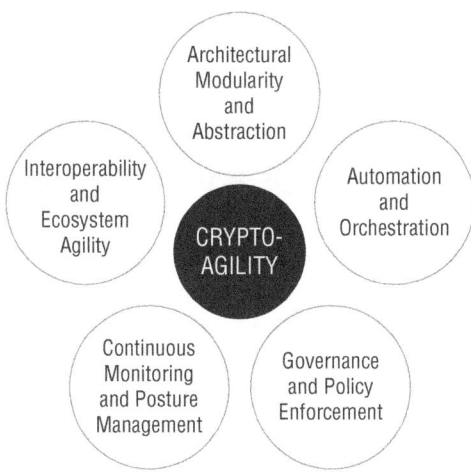

Figure 4-3: Crypto-agility principles

Ultimately, enabling crypto-agility prepares organizations not just to withstand the cryptographic challenges of the quantum era but to lead with resilience, trust, and compliance at their core.

Continuous Monitoring and Adaptation

Quantum risk is dynamic. New quantum algorithms, evolving standards, and shifting threat landscapes mean that today's secure system could be tomorrow's vulnerability. Continuous monitoring ensures that cryptographic health is maintained over time.

Organizations should integrate cryptographic monitoring into their security information and event management (SIEM) and security orchestration and automated response (SOAR) platforms, allowing real-time alerts for certificate expiration, deprecated algorithm use, and CBOM changes. Monitoring dashboards should provide executive visibility into cryptographic posture, remediation status, and compliance metrics.

Quantum computing does not simply pose a new cybersecurity threat—it forces a foundational rethink of how organizations protect their most valuable data. The time to act is now. By adopting a structured framework grounded in discovery, classification, agility, and continuous governance, business and technology leaders can manage quantum risks proactively. The investment in cryptographic resilience today will pay dividends in securing the trust, compliance, and competitive position of the organization tomorrow.

Quantum Risk Assessment: A Comprehensive Approach with Heat Maps and Maturity Models

For business and technology leaders, the challenge is not only in acknowledging the risks but also in assessing and prioritizing them with the same (or better) rigor applied to traditional threats.

This requires a comprehensive approach to quantum risk assessment. It introduces tools like heat maps to visualize risk exposure and proposes a maturity model to benchmark readiness. Using practical case examples from the banking, government, and telecommunications sectors, as well as well-grounded frameworks, this section equips leaders to evaluate their cryptographic vulnerabilities and build actionable roadmaps toward quantum resilience.

The Need for Quantum Risk Assessment

Risk assessment in the quantum context involves identifying, categorizing, and prioritizing cryptographic assets based on their exposure to quantum vulnerabilities and their business criticality. Unlike conventional cyber threats, quantum risks often pertain to future-state compromise; for example, in the HNDL scenario, data is stolen today with the intention of decrypting it when quantum computers become powerful enough [8].

Without a structured approach to quantifying this exposure, organizations risk misallocating resources, missing critical vulnerabilities, or falling out of regulatory compliance. A rigorous quantum risk assessment serves as the foundation for strategic planning, investment prioritization, and board-level decision-making.

Risk Assessment Methodology

The assessment begins by mapping discovered cryptographic assets (from CBOMs, code scans, and key inventories) to their respective business functions. Each asset is then evaluated against criteria such as algorithm strength, data sensitivity, regulatory impact, and external exposure. This multidimensional analysis enables the creation of a Quantum Risk Heat Map, as shown in Figure 4-4.

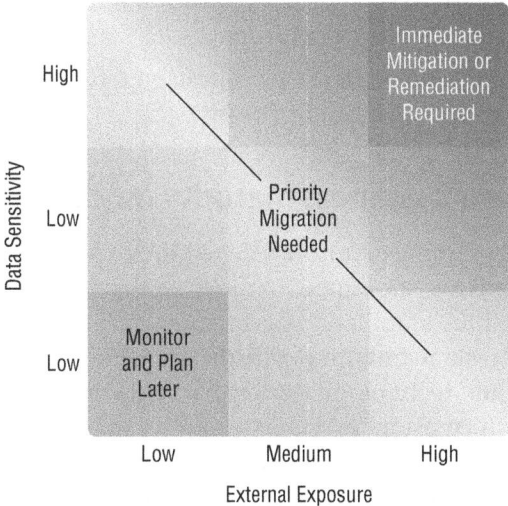

Figure 4-4: Quantum Risk Heat Map

Each quadrant of the heat map provides strategic insights:

- **High exposure and high sensitivity:** Urgent migration and remediation required
- **Low exposure and high sensitivity:** Controlled migration with strong oversight

- **High exposure and low sensitivity:** Opportunistic upgrade to reduce the attack surface

- **Low exposure and low sensitivity:** Defer action; monitor posture changes over time

Factors in Risk Scoring

Risk scoring in the quantum era is a composite evaluation across the following factors:

- **Algorithm vulnerability:** Legacy protocols such as RSA, DSA, and ECC are considered high-risk.

- **Key length and expiration:** Shorter keys with long validity periods are more exposed.

- **Application surface:** Internet-facing APIs, customer portals, and B2B interfaces increase exposure.

- **Data longevity:** Long-term sensitive data like PII, IP, and patient records requires more protection.

- **Regulatory sensitivity:** Assets under PCI-DSS, HIPAA, GDPR, and export control must be prioritized.

Quantum-Safe Readiness Maturity Model

The journey to becoming quantum safe requires a phased and disciplined approach, guided by a structured maturity model that enables enterprises to assess where they stand and chart a clear path forward. This section introduces a five-stage quantum-safe progress and maturity model that helps business and technology leaders navigate the complexity of cryptographic transformation. From no visibility to awareness, discovery, inventory, and strategy, to enterprise-wide crypto-agility architecture, automation, integrated agility, and monitoring, each level represents a critical milestone in building resilience against quantum threats [10].

The model serves as both a diagnostic framework and a strategic roadmap, enabling organizations to align their cryptographic posture with regulatory mandates, industry best practices, and evolving threat landscapes. It helps answer essential questions: What cryptographic assets are at risk? Which systems must be prioritized? How can we operationalize remediation efforts and sustain crypto-agility?

To help organizations benchmark their progress, this section describes the details of the Quantum-Safe Readiness Maturity Model shown in Figure 4-5. The model evaluates an enterprise's preparedness based on discovery, strategy, migration, agility, and monitoring.

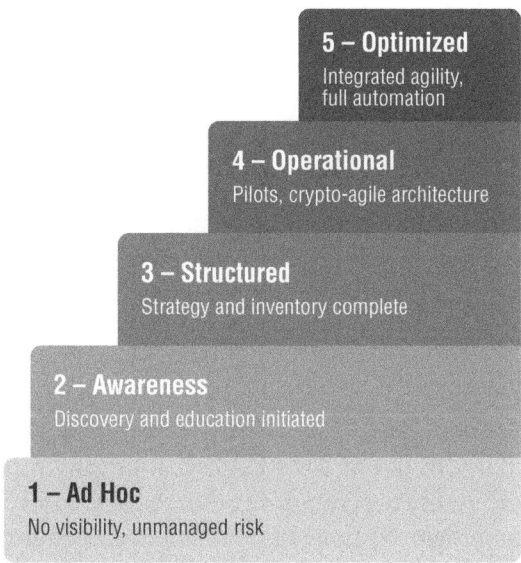

Figure 4-5: Quantum-Safe Readiness Maturity Model

Level 1 – Ad Hoc
Organizations have no visibility into their cryptographic landscape and no strategy for PQC. Risk is unmanaged.

Level 2 – Initial Awareness
Key stakeholders are informed; basic discovery is underway, typically through isolated assessments.

Level 3 – Structured Planning
Enterprise-wide CBOMs have been developed. Strategy documents and risk heat maps are in place. Tools are allocated.

Level 4 – Operational Integration
Crypto-agility principles are embedded into the architecture. PQC pilots are in progress. SIEM dashboards include crypto metrics.

Level 5 – Optimized Resilience
Automated inventory and posture monitoring is in place. PQC rollout is complete for high-risk systems. Continuous improvement processes are established.

Case Studies

Following the Quantum-Safe Readiness Maturity Model framework, here are three real-world case studies from the banking, government, and telecommunications sectors. These examples illustrate how leading institutions are applying the maturity model to drive quantum-safe readiness, transforming complexity into clarity and uncertainty into a proactive defense strategy for the quantum era.

Case Study 1: Global Bank Modernizing Transaction Security

A multinational bank with operations in 20+ countries began assessing its quantum risk after regulators emphasized post-quantum preparedness for financial institutions. The bank's internal analysis uncovered more than 4,500 digital certificates using RSA-2048 to protect customer login sessions, transaction APIs, and mobile apps.

After these were plotted on a heat map, 1,200 certificates were deemed high-risk due to their use in high-value transfers and public internet exposure. The bank initiated a hybrid cryptography pilot, deploying dual-algorithm certificates combining RSA and CRYSTALS-Kyber. It also launched training programs for developers and auditors to identify crypto-agility features in upcoming projects.

The outcome: within eight months, all externally exposed systems were upgraded with hybrid certificates, and the organization achieved Level 4 on the maturity model.

Case Study 2: National Government Enhancing Public Data Protection

A national government cybersecurity agency launched a multi-agency quantum readiness program in response to defense and critical infrastructure mandates. An audit revealed that outdated encryption protocols were being used across 65 government departments, including those managing citizen IDs, election data, and public healthcare systems.

The agency designed a centralized CBOM registry and required departments to submit quantum risk heat maps. Systems protecting long-term classified data and e-voting systems were immediately tagged for priority migration. A pilot with post-quantum VPNs and quantum-resistant Domain Name System Security Extensions (DNSSEC) was launched in collaboration with defense contractors.

By centralizing governance and funding migration projects based on heat map outputs, the agency achieved Level 3 to Level 4 progression across critical departments within a year.

Case Study 3: Telecom Leader Securing 5G Infrastructure

A leading telecom company operating across the Asia–Pacific initiated a quantum risk assessment after identifying third-party vendors using vulnerable encryption in 5G base station software. The company's inventory revealed that more than 30% of network-facing APIs used ECC and RSA keys with no agility layer.

Using the maturity model, the organization recognized that it was at Level 2 and lacked structured remediation plans. It launched an enterprise-wide quantum threat readiness project, integrating PQC support into CI/CD pipelines, upgrading certificate management systems, and introducing CBOM-based contract clauses for vendors.

Within 12 months, the company upgraded all critical communication control systems to support PQC, embedded crypto monitoring in its security operations center (SOC), and achieved Level 4 maturity, with plans to reach Level 5 by 2026.

Quantum risk assessment is a strategic imperative for today's digital enterprises. By visualizing threats through heat maps, assigning clear risk scores, and benchmarking readiness through maturity models, organizations can move from uncertainty to action. As demonstrated in these case studies, quantum risk assessments not only identify gaps but also create a roadmap to resilience.

Continuous Monitoring and Adaptation to Evolving Quantum Risks

Quantum computing is moving from theoretical potential to technological reality. As this evolution accelerates, the cyber threat landscape is undergoing a fundamental shift. Traditional encryption schemes—once considered unbreakable—are becoming vulnerable. Although a practical quantum attack may still be years away, the HNDL threat is immediate and active. In this environment, enterprises must commit to continuous monitoring and adaptive security practices. This section outlines how organizations can implement a responsive, forward-looking framework to monitor evolving quantum threats and adapt rapidly to mitigate emerging risks.

The Business Case for Continuous Monitoring

Quantum threats evolve unpredictably. Advances in quantum algorithms, hardware stability, and fault-tolerant architectures can change the threat profile overnight. This unpredictability necessitates continuous monitoring—not only of the organization's internal cryptographic health but also of the broader quantum threat landscape.

Static assessments are insufficient. Business and technology leaders must embed real-time monitoring into governance, infrastructure, and development workflows. This ensures the timely detection of cryptographic weaknesses and enables informed decisions about upgrading algorithms, certificates, and controls. As governments, including the United States and the EU, roll out post-quantum mandates, staying ahead of evolving standards becomes a compliance necessity and a competitive differentiator [4].

Key Monitoring Mechanisms

Effective quantum-era cybersecurity demands proactive visibility into emerging risks and vulnerabilities. Organizations must employ diverse monitoring mechanisms—spanning external threat intelligence, quantum-context-aware analytics, and realistic adversary simulations—to detect, assess, and address evolving cryptographic threats before they impact operations. The following approaches form the core of a resilient monitoring strategy.

Threat Intelligence Feeds

Threat intelligence helps contextualize the pace and direction of quantum computing developments. Effective programs do the following:

- Subscribe to authoritative sources (NIST, NSA, European Telecommunications Standards Institute [ETSI], Quantum Economic Development Consortium [QED-C]) for updates on PQC algorithms and vulnerabilities.
- Participate in sector-specific information sharing groups (e.g., Financial Services Information Sharing and Analysis Center

[FS-ISAC], Health Information Sharing and Analysis Center [H-ISAC]).

▪ Monitor quantum-related academic breakthroughs through journals and platforms like arXiv [11].

Incorporating these insights into security dashboards enables teams to align their defenses with emerging risks.

SIEM with Quantum Context Awareness

Traditional SIEM platforms must be upgraded to understand cryptographic telemetry. Quantum-aware SIEM systems should do the following:

▪ Identify anomalies in hybrid cryptographic operations (e.g., TLS negotiation failures involving PQC).

▪ Monitor for unusual certificate lifecycle behaviors or expired/incompatible key exchanges.

▪ Alert on potential data exfiltration patterns linked to HNDL campaigns.

Integrating quantum-aware analytics into SIEM workflows allows security teams to correlate and act on indicators early.

Red Teaming and Post-Quantum Simulations

Simulated attacks can validate the organization's quantum readiness. These exercises may include the following:

▪ Emulating HNDL exfiltration followed by delayed decryption

▪ Breaking hybrid cryptographic stacks to expose compatibility gaps

▪ Assessing outdated legacy systems vulnerable to post-quantum exploits

These drills help quantify technical debt and prioritize migration activities.

Agile Adaptation Strategies

Monitoring is only the first half. Effective quantum defense requires organizations to adapt rapidly based on insights. This demands agile policies, technical flexibility, and executive commitment.

Security Agility and DevSecOps

Crypto-agility is the ability to swap algorithms without rewriting applications. Agile security practices support this by doing the following:

- Using modular cryptographic libraries with drop-in PQC support
- Embedding cryptographic validation into DevSecOps workflows
- Enforcing compliance gates for crypto-safe deployment in CI/CD

This agility reduces the time to mitigation and ensures business continuity amid evolving threats.

Investment in Research and Open Innovation

Staying ahead requires experimentation and research. Organizations should do the following:

- Fund internal R&D or partner with academic centers for PQC testing.
- Contribute to open-source PQC tools and libraries.
- Engage in pilots like the NIST NCCoE migration projects to benchmark strategies.

Investing in innovation builds resilience and future-proofs the security stack [2].

Strategic Partnerships and Ecosystem Collaboration

Quantum safety cannot be achieved in isolation. Collaborating across the ecosystem accelerates adoption and enriches intelligence. These are some key initiatives:

- Partnering with cybersecurity vendors to validate PQC readiness
- Joining working groups such as the ETSI Quantum-Safe Task Force
- Coordinating with regulators to understand and influence compliance frameworks

Ecosystem-wide collaboration also enhances threat signal fidelity and solution interoperability [10].

Proactive Governance and Risk Oversight

C-level commitment is essential to quantum resilience. Governance enhancements include the following:

- Designating a Quantum Risk Officer or creating a cross-functional quantum task force.
- Reviewing crypto-inventory and risk posture quarterly at the board level.
- Integrating PQC migration progress into organizational KPIs and compliance scorecards.

Such measures institutionalize quantum readiness and ensure accountability.

Building a Resilient Posture

Continuous monitoring and adaptive defense are not optional in the quantum era. The quantum threat landscape will evolve faster than traditional change cycles. Organizations that institutionalize quantum awareness, invest in agility, and embed governance across their value chain will mitigate risks and gain a strategic edge.

Business and technology leaders must act now. The cost of waiting until quantum attacks materialize is far greater than the investment in preparedness today.

Regulatory Compliance in the Quantum-Safe Landscape

As quantum computing transitions from academic pursuit to emerging reality, regulatory compliance is becoming a central pillar of enterprise security strategy. The cryptographic algorithms that protect our global digital economy—RSA, ECC, and others—are increasingly vulnerable to future quantum attacks. Governments, international standards bodies, and industry-specific regulators are responding by accelerating the development of new mandates, compliance frameworks, and best practices around PQC. Business and technology leaders must act now to navigate this evolving landscape, avoid penalties, and future-proof their organizations.

Evolving Regulatory Landscape

The regulatory environment surrounding cryptography is transforming rapidly. Quantum risk is no longer a hypothetical issue; it is now recognized as a strategic and compliance risk. Regulatory initiatives are gaining momentum on multiple fronts, and organizations must monitor, interpret, and operationalize these requirements across jurisdictions and industries [9].

Global Standards and Guidelines

International standards-setting organizations are leading the charge on quantum-safe preparedness:

- **NIST (United States):** NIST's PQC standardization effort, launched in 2016, has entered its final rounds. Algorithms like CRYSTALS-Kyber (for encryption) and Dilithium (for digital signatures) are being adopted as quantum-safe standards [1].

- **ISO/IEC:** The International Organization for Standardization is developing PQC-related standards such as ISO/IEC 14888 and ISO/IEC 18033 [12].

- **ETSI:** The ETSI has launched dedicated task forces for quantum-safe cryptography [13].

Organizations that ignore these developments risk falling behind regulatory expectations and international norms.

Industry-Specific Regulations

Different sectors will face tailored quantum-safe mandates based on the sensitivity and longevity of the data they manage:

- **Financial services:** Regulators like the Basel Committee on Banking Supervision (BCBS) and the U.S. SEC are evaluating how quantum threats could affect systemic risk. Banks may soon be required to implement quantum-resilient transaction and identity protocols.

- **Healthcare:** Bodies governing health data protection, such as HIPAA in the United States and GDPR in the EU, are expected to evolve encryption and data access requirements in line with quantum threats.

- **Critical infrastructure:** Governmental agencies in defense, energy, and telecom sectors are releasing guidance requiring crypto-agility and PQC adoption for operational technologies and supply chains.

Data Protection Laws

The rise of data privacy regulation has increased pressure on organizations to secure personal data against long-term threats:

- **GDPR (EU):** Article 32 requires "appropriate technical and organizational measures." As quantum computing renders current encryption obsolete, failure to adopt PQC may be seen as noncompliance.

- **CCPA (California):** The CCPA imposes strict penalties for the mishandling of personal data. As regulators increase scrutiny, encryption methods will be evaluated for quantum resilience.

As legal interpretations evolve, quantum-safe cryptography is likely to become a mandated control for compliance with these data protection laws.

Compliance Strategies

Meeting emerging PQC compliance expectations demands a structured and proactive approach. Business and technology leaders should consider the following strategies to embed compliance into their operations.

Regular Audits and Risk Assessments

Organizations should implement periodic cryptographic posture assessments to:

- Evaluate legacy encryption deployments.
- Identify assets and systems that are vulnerable to quantum attacks.
- Establish baseline metrics for quantum readiness.

These assessments help pinpoint compliance gaps and prioritize remediation based on risk exposure.

Policy and Procedure Updates

Security and compliance policies must be updated to reflect quantum risk:

- Revise **data encryption policies** to specify acceptable PQC algorithms.
- Update **access control policies** to ensure compatibility with new certificate and key formats.
- Expand **incident response plans** to include quantum-triggered vulnerabilities or breaches.

Documented and enforced policy updates demonstrate due diligence in the face of emerging threats.

Engagement with Regulators and Standards Bodies

Active engagement with regulatory and standards communities enables organizations to:

- Gain early insight into evolving compliance expectations.
- Influence the shape of new requirements through industry consultation.
- Align internal timelines with upcoming deadlines and draft policies.

Participation in groups like ETSI, NIST working groups, and national security task forces also helps enterprises stay ahead of industry peers [12].

Third-Party Certifications and Independent Validation

Obtaining third-party validations and certifications will become increasingly important as regulators and clients demand assurance:

- Look for certifications based on emerging PQC readiness standards (e.g., ISO/IEC PQC frameworks).
- Conduct third-party audits to assess cryptographic agility, inventory quality, and implementation readiness.
- Use certification and audit results to build trust with customers and regulators [12].

Independent validation signals maturity and transparency in quantum-safe compliance.

The regulatory landscape around PQC is expanding rapidly, driven by increasing awareness of quantum threats and the critical need for crypto-agility. Compliance is not merely a technical requirement: it is becoming a business imperative tied to trust, data protection, and digital sovereignty.

Business and technology leaders must develop adaptive compliance strategies that include standards alignment, sector-specific readiness, regular audits, and proactive engagement with regulators. Those who act now will avoid penalties and position their organizations as trusted digital stewards in the quantum computing world.

As quantum computing continues to evolve, so do the risks it poses to cybersecurity. Managing these risks requires a comprehensive approach that includes identifying potential threats, building robust risk management frameworks, ensuring regulatory compliance, conducting thorough risk assessments, and continuously monitoring and adapting to new developments. By staying proactive and prepared, organizations can safeguard their assets and operations against the challenges of the quantum era.

Summary

This chapter covered the nuances of managing cyber risks in the post-quantum era. It provided a comprehensive framework for identifying, assessing, mitigating, and monitoring these new threats.

References

(1) NIST, Post-Quantum Cryptography, https://csrc.nist.gov/projects/post-quantum-cryptography.

(2) NIST, Migration to Post-Quantum Cryptography, https://www.nccoe.nist.gov/projects/building-blocks/post-quantum-cryptography.

(3) NSA, CNSA 2.0 Fact Sheet, https://media.defense.gov/2022/Sep/07/2003071836/-1/-1/0/CSI_CNSA_2.0_FAQ_.PDF.

(4) ENISA, Post-Quantum Guidance, https://www.enisa.europa.eu/publications/post-quantum-cryptography.

(5) ISO/IEC 27005:2022, Information Security Risk Management, `https://www.iso.org/standard/80585.html`.

(6) IBM, Quantum Safe, `https://www.ibm.com/quantum/quantum-safe`.

(7) World Economic Forum, Quantum Threat Report, `https://www.weforum.org/agenda/2023/02/quantum-computing-cybersecurity-threat`.

(8) Gartner Post-Quantum Cryptography: The Time to Prepare is Now! `https://www.gartner.com/en/documents/5550295`.

(9) NSA, Cybersecurity Advisory on Quantum-Readiness `https://media.defense.gov/2023/Aug/21/2003284212/-1/-1/0/CSI-QUANTUM-READINESS.PDF`.

(10) World Economic Forum, Transitioning to a Quantum-Secure Economy, `https://www.weforum.org/publications/transitioning-to-a-quantum-secure-economy`.

(11) arXiv, recent quantum physics papers, `https://arxiv.org/list/quant-ph/recent`.

(12) ISO/IEC, quantum cryptography standards, `https://www.iso.org`.

(13) ETSI, Quantum-Safe Cryptography, `https://www.etsi.org/technologies/quantum-safe-cryptography`.

Implementing Quantum-Safe Solutions to Protect Your Business

"It's very hard to secure a system that's been built on the assumption that certain problems are hard, once those problems become easy."

—Ron Rivest

Although no one knows exactly when Q-Day (the day when quantum computing will be able to break current cryptographic standards) will arrive, most sources indicate that it is coming sooner than initially thought. For example, Professor Michele Mosca of the Institute for Quantum Computing at the University of Waterloo estimates that there is a one-in-seven chance that some of the asymmetric cryptographic algorithms our digital world depends on today will be broken by 2026 and a 50% chance by 2031 [1].

Figure 5-1 shows three critical dates. First is the date when Peter Shor proved that the mathematical problems underpinning today's public-key cryptographic standards (e.g., Diffie-Hellman [DH], Rivest-Shamir-Adleman [RSA], and elliptic curve cryptography [ECC]) can be broken by quantum computing. Next is the current day, when sensitive data protected with today's public-key cryptographic standards is vulnerable to "harvest now and decrypt later" (HNDL) attacks. Finally, there is Q-Day, when today's public-key cryptographic standards will be broken and any previously harvested HNDL data can be decrypted.

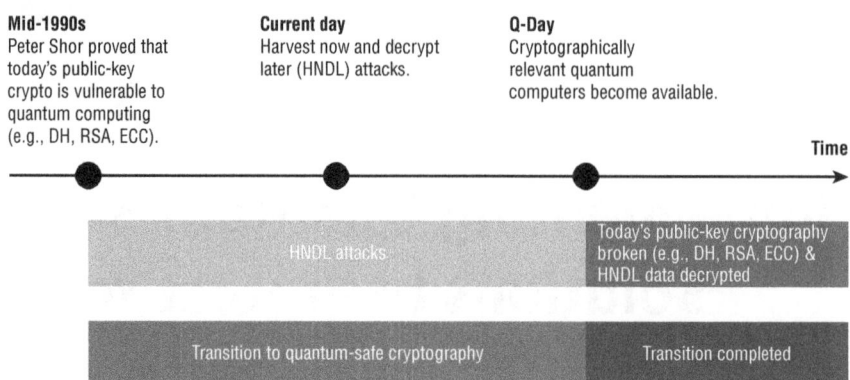

Figure 5-1: Timeline for transitioning to quantum-safe cryptography

In this chapter, we show why it is critical to start preparing for transitioning to quantum-safe cryptography *now*. Next, we introduce a prescriptive approach for guiding organizations in their transition to quantum-safe cryptography. Finally, we discuss a real-world example of transitioning a major software product to quantum-safe cryptography.

The Urgency of Transitioning to Quantum-Safe Cryptography

Transitioning to quantum-safe cryptography is not only a business imperative to secure data and infrastructure but also an urgent endeavor that must begin *now*. There are two primary reasons for this urgency. First, HNDL attacks are already putting sensitive data at risk. And second, the task of updating cryptographic implementations to become quantum safe is anything but simple. This change is much more profound than any cryptographic update we have seen before.

The Harvest Now and Decrypt Later Problem

The HNDL problem is probably the most important reason it is so critical to start preparing now to transition to quantum-safe cryptography. HNDL attacks may be happening today, and valuable secrets may already be in the hands of threat actors. For example, in 2016, Canadian Internet traffic destined for South Korea was mysteriously rerouted via China. This rerouting lasted approximately six months, indicating that it was not an innocent glitch [2]. Similar incidents have been reported many times around the world. For example, in 2019, an incident was reported that affected a substantial amount of European mobile traffic [2]. Also, in 2020, data from Google, Amazon, Facebook, and more than 200 networks was mysteriously redirected through Russia [2].

HNDL attacks do not affect data at rest. Instead, they target data communications, specifically when data with a long-term value is exchanged. Examples of potential targets include the following:

- **Military Services:** Communications involving highly confidential data, such as military equipment design plans

- **Intelligence Agencies:** As with military services, communications involving highly confidential data, such as the names and locations of agents located overseas

- **Personal Data Handlers:** Communications involving personally identifiable information (PII), such as healthcare data, which government regulations mandate must be protected for extended periods of 5, 10, or 20 years or more

HNDL attacks target data communications because their underlying protocols use asymmetric cryptographic algorithms, which are not quantum safe. For example, consider the scenario illustrated in Figure 5-2, where two agencies are exchanging highly confidential data over a communication channel protected with Transport Layer Security (TLS). As we saw in Chapter 3, TLS uses asymmetric cryptographic algorithms such as RSA in its handshake phase. If a threat actor harvests the data exchanged between these two agencies, they will be able to break RSA when Q-Day arrives and therefore derive the RSA private key used. Armed with this private key, they will then be able to easily decrypt the data exchanged and uncover the secrets.

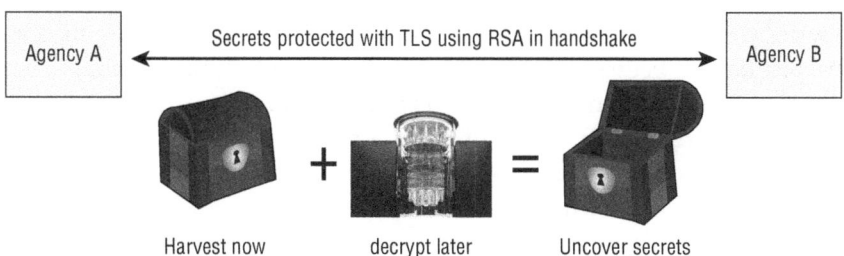

Figure 5-2: Harvest now and decrypt later.

The Challenges of Updating the Cryptographic Landscape

At first glance, transitioning to quantum-safe cryptography may seem like a simple exercise in which a set of quantum-vulnerable cryptographic algorithms is replaced by an alternate set of cryptographic algorithms that are quantum safe. Unfortunately, this is not the case. The reason it is not a simple exercise is that changing cryptographic algorithms requires more than code changes to perform the swap. First, quantum-vulnerable cryptographic algorithms need to be identified across the enterprise IT environment in all applications, databases, operating systems, and IT infrastructure components where cryptography is used. Next, dependencies need to be identified, such as the cryptographic libraries underpinning the cryptography used in the IT environment. Understanding these dependencies is key to planning any transition to quantum-safe cryptography because code changes cannot happen until the providers of the cryptographic libraries ship newer versions that include quantum-safe cryptographic algorithms.

Additionally, new certificates signed with the new quantum-safe algorithms need to be issued so that they can be used to secure software distribution, system authentication, and data communications. There are also differences in key sizes and signature lengths between quantum-vulnerable cryptographic algorithms and quantum-safe ones. These differences will most likely have a significant impact on the implementation efforts to use the new algorithms. Finally, new skills in quantum-safe cryptography and associated primitives need to be built to execute the transition.

Besides these challenges, history shows that updating cryptographic implementations takes time. For example, the Heartbleed vulnerability was introduced into the OpenSSL cryptographic library in 2012. It was discovered and subsequently fixed in 2014. But five years later, 200,000 devices were still unpatched. Another example is the SHA-3 hash function. Despite having been selected by NIST in 2012, SHA-3 still has not gained widespread adoption today. ECC is another cryptographic algorithm that took a long time from its introduction until it began to be adopted. ECC was introduced back in 1985, and only after two decades did it gain widespread adoption.

Clearly, transitioning to quantum-safe cryptography is no simple task. It is a much more profound change to cryptographic implementations than anything we have seen in the past. This, coupled with the HNDL threat, makes transitioning to quantum-safe cryptography both urgent and a business imperative to secure data and infrastructure.

A Prescriptive Approach for Transitioning to Quantum-Safe Cryptography

Transitioning to quantum-safe cryptography is a major endeavor and needs to be carefully planned and executed. In this section, we describe a prescriptive approach to guide organizations through their journey to quantum-safe cryptography. This prescriptive approach consists of the following five steps:

Step 1: Discover the Cryptographic Inventory

Discovery is the first step in the journey to transitioning to quantum-safe cryptography. The primary objective of the Discover step is to provide visibility into the cryptographic landscape used across the organization's entire IT environment. This includes the cryptographic libraries and algorithms used in applications, the cipher suites used by network endpoints, the encryption key sizes used to secure data and communications, and the digital certificates used to authenticate systems, secure communications, and sign digital assets.

The success of the discovery process depends on two key aspects: tooling and standardization. Tooling helps automate the discovery of cryptographic assets and the identification of any vulnerabilities. Standardization enables this tooling to more easily reason about cryptographic assets and their dependencies, such as checking for compliance with policies that apply to the use of cryptography in applications. The Cryptography Bill of Materials (CBOM) standard was introduced specifically for this purpose. It is an extension of the CycloneDX standard for the Software Bill of Materials (SBOM), with concepts to model cryptographic assets [3]. The key objective of CBOM is to provide an abstraction that allows the representation of cryptographic assets in a structured object format. This representation includes the following:

- **Modeling Cryptographic Assets:** The cryptographic assets that need to be modeled include cryptographic algorithms, cryptographic protocols, and digital certificates.

■ **Capturing Cryptographic Asset Properties:** Certain cryptographic assets have properties that also need to be modeled. For example, modeling a cryptographic algorithm such as AES is not sufficient. It is equally important to model the mode in which such an algorithm (e.g., Cipher Block Chaining [CBC], Galois/Counter Mode [GCM]) is used because the security level of the algorithm also depends on the mode in which an application uses it.

■ **Capturing Cryptographic Asset Dependencies:** A CBOM tracks two types of dependencies to better understand the impact of a cryptographic asset. The first is implementation: for example, a cryptographic library implements certain algorithms or protocols. The second type of dependency is usage: for example, an application uses a given algorithm from a cryptographic library.

Figure 5-3 shows a CBOM modeling the usage of the AES cryptographic algorithm in GCM mode and with a 128-bit key size.

```
"components": [
...
  {
    "type": "crypto-asset",
    "bom-ref": "oid:2.16.840.1.101.3.4.1.6",
    "name": "AES",
    "cryptoProperties": {
        "assetType": "algorithm",
        "algorithmProperties": {
            "variant": "AES-128-GCM",
            "primitive": "ae",
            "mode": "gcm",
            "implementationLevel": "softwarePlainRam",
            "implementationPlatform": "x86_64",
            "certificationLevel": "none",
            "cryptoFunctions": ["keygen", "encrypt", "decrypt", "tag"]
        }
        "classicalSecurityLevel": 128,
        "nistQuantumSecurityLevel": 1
    }
  }
...
]
```

Figure 5-3: CBOM modeling

Step 2: Assess the Risk and Prioritize Remediation

The objective of this step is to look for vulnerabilities across the cryptographic inventory discovered in Step 1. We believe that the need to transition to quantum-safe encryption provides an excellent opportunity to modernize encryption implementations overall. Therefore, the vulnerabilities discovered by this step are not limited to usages of algorithms that are not quantum safe but should include any cryptographic vulnerabilities. These cryptographic vulnerabilities can be divided into two main categories. The first category represents vulnerabilities that can be addressed without requiring an application change. They include expired encryption keys that must be rotated, expired certificates that must be renewed, keystores for which file permissions must be restricted, and so on. The second category represents vulnerabilities that require an application change to fix them. For example, an application that creates digital signatures using RSA must be changed to use a quantum-safe alternative such as Module-Lattice-Based Digital Signature Algorithm (ML-DSA). Similarly, an application that establishes a key exchange protocol using DH must be changed to use a quantum-safe alternative such as Module-Lattice-Based Key-Encapsulation Mechanism (ML-KEM).

Although uncovering cryptographic vulnerabilities is important, risk-based prioritization is equally important so that the organization can focus first on the issues with the highest risk. Enrichment data is required to perform this risk-based prioritization. Consider the following example: two databases, A and B, are encrypted with two encryption keys, K1 and K2, that must be rotated. Additionally, suppose that K1 and K2 are stored in a local keystore for which the file permissions must be restricted. Which issue should the organization address first: the issue for database A or database B? It is hard to tell without enrichment data. Suppose that database A contains classified information, whereas database B contains public information. This data classification information is an example of enrichment data. Risk-based prioritization can leverage this additional context to prioritize fixing the issue for database A first because it poses a greater risk for the organization.

Step 3: Design a Crypto-Agile Architecture

Migration to quantum-safe cryptography is both a challenge and an opportunity. It is a challenge because it requires applications to be changed so that new quantum-safe algorithms are used instead of the quantum-vulnerable ones. This, as we have discussed, is a tremendous endeavor. But it is also an opportunity to modernize how applications consume cryptography. In fact, by consuming cryptography as a service, we decouple the application from the underlying cryptographic library, enabling the cryptography to be updated with few or no changes to the application.

Under this new crypto-agile architecture, applications will be changed to use an SDK that provides an abstract set of cryptographic APIs (e.g., Generate Key, Encrypt, Decrypt, Verify, Sign), and the implementation of this API will reside in a new system that provides cryptography as a service. This system will use a plurality of cryptographic libraries, and each application will have a profile defined within this system that specifies, among other things, the cryptographic library currently used by the application.

Suppose that a vulnerability is discovered in a cryptographic library currently used by an application. This issue could be addressed with virtually no changes to the application by simply updating the application's profile to use a non-vulnerable cryptographic library. Figure 5-4 illustrates this method for applying cryptography to future-proof applications against changes to cryptographic standards and cryptographic vulnerabilities.

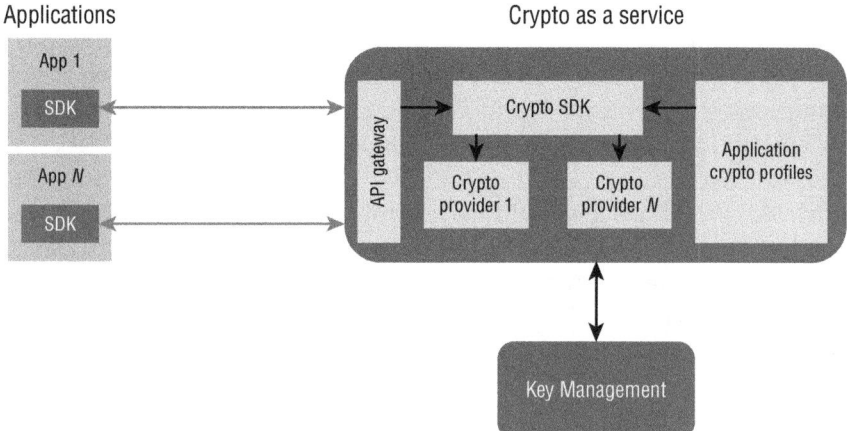

Figure 5-4: Cryptography as a service

Step 4: Migrate to Quantum-Safe Cryptography

The primary objective of this step is to make the actual changes to the IT environment to become quantum safe. These changes can be divided into three categories: operational changes, mitigation changes, and strategic changes.

Operational changes are the lowest-hanging fruit. They include tasks such as updating a cryptographic library to a newer version that includes the new quantum-safe algorithms. They may also include rotating encryption keys or renewing digital certificates before they expire.

Mitigation changes are more complex, and they aim to address two major challenges. The first is the HNDL challenge. As we discussed earlier, sensitive data is already at risk now, so organizations are looking for ways to mitigate this vulnerability sooner rather than later. The second challenge is the fact that some legacy applications may not be able to change to become quantum safe, perhaps because the code is too old or because it is too expensive to change. But this creates a problem because these legacy applications will not be able to service clients that are already quantum safe. Similarly, some legacy clients may not be able to change to become quantum safe, yet there is a business need for them to continue to interact with applications. So, how can all these challenges be overcome? This is where an adaptive proxy solution helps. An *adaptive proxy solution* allows quantum-safe clients to interact with quantum-safe applications normally. But it can also dynamically terminate a TLS connection and re-establish a new one with a quantum-safe client to securely interact with a non-quantum-safe application and vice versa. The adaptive proxy can be intelligently placed close to the application or client (depending on the scenario) to ensure secure data communications. Figure 5-5 depicts the high-level architecture of an adaptive proxy.

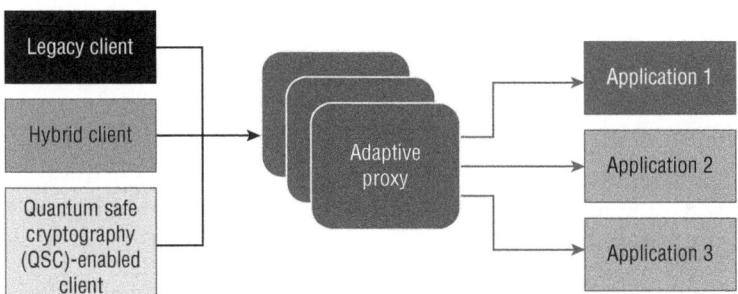

Figure 5-5: Adaptive proxy high-level architecture

Strategic changes are about changing application code to use the new quantum-safe algorithms instead of non-quantum-safe ones. This presents an opportunity to modernize how applications consume cryptography by adopting a crypto-agile architecture as described in step 3.

Step 5: Ongoing Monitoring, Compliance, and Adaptation

The primary objective of this step is to continuously assess the cryptographic security and compliance posture of the IT environment. We refer to this continuous process as cryptographic posture management (CPM). Tooling is critical for the successful implementation of such a process. A successful CPM tool must provide the following minimum set of capabilities:

- **Integration with Cryptographic Discovery Tools:** The CPM tool must provide for ingesting cryptographic inventories from various discovery tools such as source code scanners, object code scanners, and network scanners.

- **Prebuilt and Custom Compliance Policies:** The CPM tool must include prebuilt policies that enable organizations to understand where their cryptographic posture stands with respect to known cryptographic standards, such as those from NIST. Additionally, the observability tool must allow organizations to define their own cryptographic policies to meet their specific needs. For example, one organization may have a more restrictive policy than another regarding older versions of certain cryptographic libraries.

- **Prioritization:** The CPM tool must help organizations prioritize remediation tasks. One aspect of this is risk-based prioritization, discussed in step 2. But equally important is dependency analysis. This is critical to allow organizations to gain visibility into any constraints that may impact remediation. For example, fixing a non-quantum-safe usage in an application may not be immediately possible because there is a dependency on a cryptographic library used by a dependent component for which the vendor has not yet provided a quantum-safe version.

- **Integration with Remediation Systems:** The CPM tool must enable organizations to trigger actions on prioritized risks. For example, an integration with a ticketing system such as ServiceNow will allow the organization to automatically open a ticket for a given risk so it is addressed by the appropriate team. Similarly, an integration with an operational cryptographic system will allow the organization to automatically trigger a remediation. For example, an integration with a key management system (KMS) will let the organization automatically trigger an encryption key rotation.

Case Study: Transitioning IBM DB2 to Quantum-Safe Cryptography

IBM DB2 is a major database system relied on by thousands of customers worldwide. It is a client-server architecture in which a database client, such as JDBC, issues requests (e.g., SQL) and a database server receives those requests, processes them, and returns a response (e.g., query results set) to the database client. DB2 provides a comprehensive set of security capabilities that customers depend on to meet their security and compliance mandates. Our analysis of the DB2 source code shows that IBM Global Security Kit (GSKit) is the library providing all the cryptographic services for DB2, including an implementation of the TLS protocol. It also shows that the GSKit cryptographic functions are used by the following DB2 capabilities:

- **User Authentication:** DH is used during this process to allow the database client and the database server to agree on a session key.
- **Transparent Data Encryption:** AES-256 is used for database encryption. Both the data encryption keys (DEKs) and the key encryption keys (KEKs) are AES-256 keys.
- **TLS:** Different cipher suites are supported for securing the communication between the database client and database server, including RSA and ECC.

Transparent data encryption is already quantum-safe because AES-256 is used exclusively for this purpose. User authentication and TLS, on the other hand, are not quantum safe because they use quantum-vulnerable algorithms such as DH, ECC, and RSA. This proof of concept (PoC) [4] of a quantum-safe DB2 authentication and quantum-safe DB2 TLS was carried out before NIST selected the quantum-safe algorithms for standardization and, obviously, before higher-level protocols such as TLS were updated to incorporate new algorithms. Therefore, the PoC opted for a hybrid model to ensure a secure implementation.

Making DB2 User Authentication Quantum Safe

When a user authenticates to DB2, the DB2 client and the DB2 server need to agree on a session key before the user ID and password are sent by the client to the server for validation. Figure 5-6 illustrates this process and can be summarized as follows:

1. The DB2 client and DB2 server agree on a shared secret key (ss) using DH.

2. The DB2 client encrypts the user ID and password using the agreed-on key (ss).

3. The DB2 server decrypts the user ID and password using that same key (ss).

4. The usual authentication process follows whereby the provided user ID and password are validated by the configured authentication method for the DB2 server (e.g., operating system or LDAP).

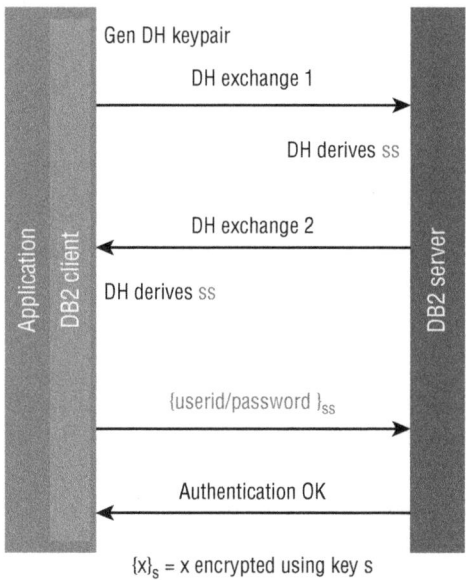

Figure 5-6: DB2 user authentication process

To make DB2 user authentication quantum-safe, we opted for a hybrid model where DH is wrapped inside ML-KEM (formerly known as CRYSTALS-Kyber). This combination of the new algorithm (ML-KEM) and the old algorithm (DH) is safe because it ensures that authentication remains within the safety of one algorithm should the second one be broken. Figure 5-7 illustrates how this hybrid implementation works and can be summarized as follows:

1. The DB2 client generates a private/public ML-KEM key pair and sends the public key to the server.

2. The server takes the public key and uses a random seed to derive a shared key (kss) and ciphertext.

3. The client uses the private key and ciphertext to derive the same shared key (kss).

4. The DB2 authentication process uses the ML-KEM shared secret as an AES-256 key to encrypt the DH key exchange.

5. The DB2 authentication process uses DH normally over this protected channel.

6. The DB2 authentication process changes the key used on the protected channel to the key from DH (dhss) to encrypt the user ID and password.

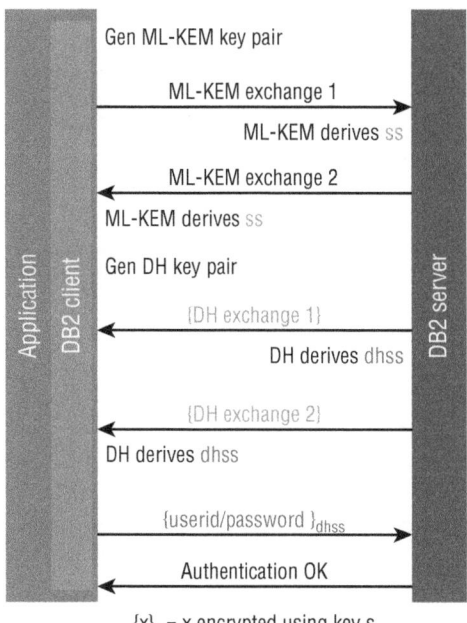

Figure 5-7: Quantum-safe DB2 user authentication process

Making DB2 TLS Quantum Safe

To make DB2 TLS quantum-safe, we opted for a hybrid model both for the TLS handshake and for digital certificate management. For the TLS handshake, we leveraged the Application-Layer Protocol Negotiation (ALPN) TLS extension to force a TLS handshake using the ML-KEM quantum-safe algorithm. For certificate management, the solution adopted, depicted in Figure 5-8, takes an existing GSKit keystore containing an existing certificate chain signed with RSA or ECDSA and transparently creates a synonymous chain that has ML-DSA (formerly known as CRYSTALS-Dilithium) signatures instead; it then binds these ML-DSA certificates to the original set via hash values of the original set. Both extensions are implemented in IBM GSKit, thus enabling not only DB2 but any GSKit consumer to experiment with quantum-safe TLS.

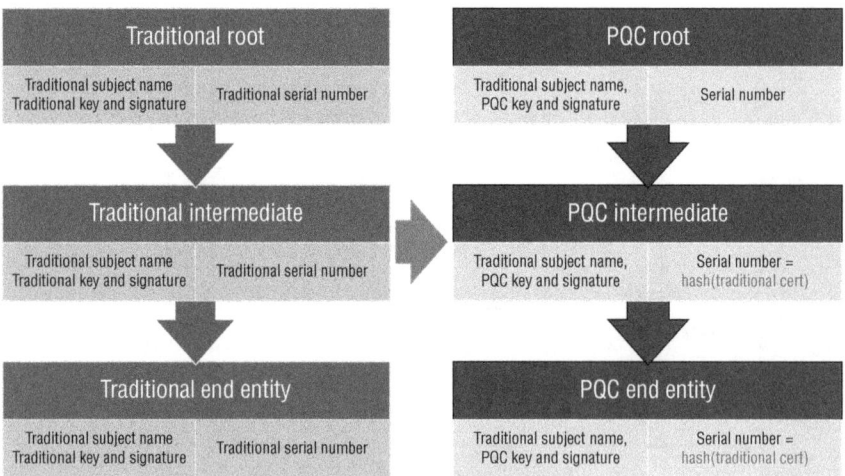

Figure 5-8: Chaining classical and quantum-safe certificates

Performance Evaluation

We ran the DB2 CONNECT command from a JDBC client to connect to the database server. This command naturally triggers both TLS-based communication and user authentication (involving the hybrid ML-KEM/ML-DSA approach discussed previously). To evaluate the performance of ML-KEM, we adopted the Monte Carlo method to repeat this test 1,000 times with both ML-KEM and DH, respectively. The average response time with ML-KEM was 0.162514 seconds (standard deviation 0.0152814 seconds). The average response time with DH was 0.163552 seconds (standard deviation 0.01222165 seconds). This data shows that the performance difference between ML-KEM and DH is very small. This performance evaluation was conducted on a test bed with 32 CPUs (1.2 GHz) and 256 GB of memory.

Summary

This chapter emphasized the urgent need for organizations to transition to quantum-safe cryptography in anticipation of Q-Day: the day when quantum computers will be able to break today's public-key cryptographic standards. We began by introducing the threat of Harvest Now and Decrypt Later (HNDL) attacks, where encrypted data is collected today and decrypted in the future using a cryptographically relevant quantum computer. Then we outlined a prescriptive five-step approach for transitioning to quantum-safe cryptography: discovering cryptographic assets, assessing risk and prioritizing remediation, designing a crypto-agile architecture, implementing changes, and enabling ongoing monitoring through cryptographic posture management (CPM). Next, a real-world case study involving IBM DB2 illustrated how quantum-safe authentication and TLS can be implemented using hybrid models that combine classical and post-quantum algorithms. Finally, we underscored that transitioning to quantum-safe cryptography is complex but critical to safeguard our digital world and maintain the confidentiality and integrity of long-term data.

References

(1) Global Risk Institute, "Quantum Computing: A New Threat to Cybersecurity," `https://globalriskinstitute.org/publication/quantum-computing-cybersecurity`.

(2) Tech Monitor, "Are harvest now, decrypt later cyberattacks actually happening?" `https://techmonitor.ai/hardware/quantum/harvest-now-decrypt-later-cyberattack-quantum-computer`.

(3) IBM Research, "IBM's Cryptography Bill of Materials to speed up quantum-safe assessment."

(4) L. Zhang, A. Miranskyy, W. Rjaibi, G. Stager, M. Gray, J. Peck, "Making Existing Software Quantum Safe: A Case Study on IBM DB2," in *Information and Software Technology Journal* 161, 2023.

Chapter X

Ensuring a Successful Transition to Quantum Safe

"Vision without action is a daydream.
Action without vision is just passing time.
Vision with action can change the world."

—Japanese Proverb

The previous chapter presented a prescriptive approach for transitioning to quantum-safe cryptography. Following such an approach is necessary but not sufficient to ensure success. This chapter presents pragmatic approaches and guidance for what enterprises should do to ensure a successful transition to becoming quantum-safe. It includes a set of potential pitfalls and fallacies, suggests approaches to avoid them, shares experiential suggestions on what other enterprises around the world are doing, and highlights how any enterprise can develop a pragmatic, fit-for-purpose roadmap to follow during its journey to becoming quantum safe.

Building a Quantum-Safe Transition Roadmap

Ensuring a successful transition to quantum-safe cryptography involves comprehensive planning and collaboration. In addition to following a prescriptive and repeatable approach, enterprises should address a variety of other aspects to ensure a successful transition. Enterprises should begin by conducting thorough risk assessments and inventorying cryptographic assets. This knowledge should be used to engage stakeholders and secure executive buy-in, which is crucial for the successful quantum-safe transformation of the enterprise. Teams will need to invest in training and upskilling staff, while staying informed about emerging standards from bodies like the National Institute of Standards and Technology (NIST). When commencing the quantum-safe transition, enterprises may implement hybrid solutions initially, conducting pilot tests to evaluate performance and compatibility. Throughout this process, they should collaborate with industry consortia, research institutions, and vendors to stay at the forefront of developments. Continuous monitoring, regular audits, and adapting to regulatory changes will ensure a robust and future-proof quantum-safe strategy.

These steps are collectively referred to here as the *quantum-safe roadmap,* and we will enumerate and discuss them in detail. They should be considered while developing a transition plan for execution.

Awareness and Education

Recognizing the impending challenges posed by quantum computing to classical cryptography, along with the urgency and complexity of the quantum-safe transition, is extremely critical. Awareness of the difficulties involved and the potential business risk of delaying must be realized at multiple levels within the enterprise:

- **Educate stakeholders.** Ensure that all relevant stakeholders, including the board, senior C-level executives, IT personnel, and security teams, understand the implications of quantum computing for cybersecurity.

- **Stay informed.** Keep abreast of developments in quantum computing and post-quantum cryptography (PQC) through industry reports, conferences, and collaboration with academic and research institutions.

Business Risk Assessment and Planning

In the previous chapter, we discussed assessing risk and prioritizing actions for remediation. Although we focused on risk based on cryptographic inventory, it is equally important to assess risk at a business level to provide much-needed business context for technical risk assessment and prioritization:

- **Business component inventory:** Identify all business components based on business process analysis or well-known business modeling exercises such as component business modeling (CBM) [1]. Leverage industry-standard frameworks and models such as the Banking Industry Architecture Network (BIAN), enhanced Telecom Operations Map (eTOM), Association of Retail Technology Standards (ARTS), and Association for Cooperative Operations Research and Development (ACORD).

- **Assess risk**: Evaluate the relative risk of these components based on:
  - Sensitive data they process
  - The type of cryptography they use currently
  - Exposure of these components to potential threat vectors
  - Business and reputational risk elements

Business Dependency Analysis

Any dynamic enterprise can be viewed as a set of interacting business components, each with well-defined processes, functional aspects, and systems that enable or execute these functions. By extension, we can infer that these business components depend on each other, and that a business process is the sequential execution of a selected subset of these business components. Understanding these dependencies is important because if an enterprise attempts to execute an end-to-end quantum-safe transformation of a business process or system, the dependent systems and components also need to be made quantum safe. Note that some business processes interact with external third-party components or systems, and these have an external dependency to consider:

- **Develop a business component-level dependency map.** Identify all business components, as mentioned earlier, and document their interdependencies. Do not forget to include third-party or external components.

- **Add cryptographic risk-based attributions.** Attach cryptographic risk assessment scores to the component-level dependency map. Doing so provides a clear representation of not only the prioritization of the components from a business risk perspective but also their interdependencies.

Technical Dependency Analysis

Cryptography is deeply embedded in systems. Cryptographic algorithms are often abstracted or hidden within libraries, APIs, middleware, cloud services, hardware security modules (HSMs), and third-party tools, among other places. A change in one part of the system will have an impact on other parts of the system or application. Having a clear understanding of these technical dependencies is critical for the successful migration of applications or systems:

- **Build a comprehensive cryptographic inventory, and map its dependencies.** Understanding all these dependencies is essential to ensure you're not overlooking components that rely on vulnerable cryptographic algorithms. Dependency analysis helps identify interconnected components that may also need to be upgraded, patched, or tested together.

- **Understand third-party supply chain risk.** Many systems rely on external vendors, cloud providers, SDKs, or open-source software. Analyzing dependencies will help identify which providers or vendors need to support PQC, their plans to accomplish this, their timeline, and the impact on the enterprise's systems and applications.

Enabling Cryptographic Agility

One of the main challenges in executing a quantum-safe transition effectively is that cryptography has evolved over the years to become pervasive and deeply embedded in our applications and systems. As enterprises transition from classic cryptography implementations to PQC implementations, it is vital to implement these new algorithms in a modular fashion, so we know where they reside and they can be changed or updated later with minimal or no disruption to business functionality. Enabling such crypto-agility is a critical topic, and we will delve into it more deeply in the next chapter:

- **Locate specific uses of cryptography.** In addition to building an inventory of what cryptography is used in systems across the enterprise, it is also vital to capture where specifically it is used. Typical software applications have cryptography-related source code distributed across several components. Knowing all these locations and the specific pattern of cryptographic usage is important.

- **Develop modularization approaches**: An inventory of specific usage patterns leads to the ability to create modular designs for PQC implementation. This forethought and design will result in significant benefits during implementation, testing, and subsequent updates if needed.

Evaluating Quantum-Safe Algorithms

Migration from classic cryptography to PQC has been likened to the Y2K problem of going from a two-digit year to a four-digit year. This comparison, although reasonable in communicating the vastness of the impact, does not hold up when it comes to comparing the complexity of the changes involved. Classical algorithms are set up and invoked differently than PQC algorithms. Thus the transition to PQC algorithms is not a one-for-one replacement during implementation. Therefore, it is important to determine how implementing the new algorithms will impact the applications in an enterprise. Understanding the new algorithm's dynamic performance characteristics is a prerequisite for any successful transition to becoming quantum safe:

- **Review standards and usage guidelines.** Follow recommendations and standards from bodies like NIST, which evaluate and standardize PQC algorithms. Analyzing the usage guidelines from the standards bodies is also critical.

- **Select appropriate algorithms.** Choose quantum-safe algorithms that meet your organization's security requirements and are compatible with existing systems where possible. Leverage performance benchmarking capabilities where available, test the new algorithms in your environment, and compare their performance in your organization to published benchmarks [2, 3].

Proofs of Concept and Pilots

Before embarking on a large-scale transformation or transition, it is prudent to identify specific aspects of the transition that need to be proven or validated, or for which the organization needs to gain experience.

Executing a very focused and targeted set of proofs of concept (PoCs) as well as pilots is a great way to accomplish that:

- **Implement PoCs.** Test the selected usage scenarios of quantum-safe algorithms in the context of applications. This differs from testing algorithms, as mentioned earlier, in that you not only test the algorithms but also observe them in operation in the context of an end-to-end business use case.

- **Conduct pilot projects.** Expand the PoC work to larger pilot projects, starting with noncritical systems to identify potential issues and assess performance impacts at the use-case level.

Integration and Migration

As part of the pilot projects and PoCs, consider the effect of starting with a hybrid approach and then moving to exclusively using PQC algorithms. Also use available third-party systems and integrations:

- **Update cryptographic libraries.** Integrate quantum-safe algorithms into your cryptographic libraries and software development kits (SDKs).

- **Use a hybrid approach.** Consider using a hybrid approach initially, where quantum-safe algorithms are used alongside classical algorithms to ensure backward compatibility and a gradual transition.

Testing and Validation

While executing the transition to quantum safe cryptography is itself a critical activity, testing and validating that all the transition steps have been successfully executed without the introduction of any new errors is an even more critical activity. This also consumes a good portion of the efforts and therefore budget needs to be allocated towards the transition. Some of the key elements that need to be tested and validated are:

- **Test third-party components:** Perform extensive testing to ensure that the new quantum-safe systems function correctly and securely. Although this can be accomplished on all custom and internal applications maintained and managed by the enterprise, it is very difficult when it comes to testing and validating third-party provider systems and services. This is where a testing mechanism based on dependency maps becomes valuable.

■ **Validate and certify for compliance:** It is also a good idea to seek validation and certification from recognized bodies to ensure compliance with industry standards and best practices.

Training and Development

Migration to PQC is a journey that takes several years. This requires careful planning and execution, as we have mentioned throughout this book. It is only natural, therefore, for the personnel involved in the migration effort, directly and indirectly, to be trained on the necessary aspects of this transition and ongoing support of the migrated systems:

■ **Train staff.** Provide training for IT and security personnel on the following:

  ■ Nuances of the most effective use of the newer PQC algorithms

  ■ Implementation of these algorithms in systems and their integration with third parties

  ■ Ongoing maintenance of quantum-safe cryptographic systems

  ■ Best practices for responding to threats or vulnerabilities

■ **Develop expertise.** Encourage continuous learning and development in the field of PQC.

Continuous Monitoring and Improvement

As we emphasized earlier, classic cryptography has evolved over the past five decades, has been incrementally included in IT systems, and is now pervasive. However, due to the way it has evolved, it has also become very difficult to manage effectively, let alone efficiently. The transition to PQC presents a unique opportunity to implement mechanisms to ensure ongoing management and maintenance of the enterprise's cryptographic posture:

■ **Monitor systems.** Continuously monitor systems for vulnerabilities and performance issues related to new cryptographic implementations.

- **Ensure up-to-date compliance.** Keep systems updated with the latest patches and improvements in quantum-safe cryptographic algorithms and practices.

- **Use policy-based management.** Manage the enterprise's cryptographic posture based on robust policies, and ensure that these policies are applied through posture management systems. Identify violations against policies, initiate remedial actions, and track them through completion.

Change Management

As mentioned earlier, becoming quantum safe takes several years. Almost every system used by the enterprise is affected, and therefore all users are impacted either directly or indirectly. This journal must be managed like a large transformation project that spans several systems and takes several years. Change management is a critical component of any large transformation initiative:

- **Communicate regularly:** Maintain clear and consistent communication about the goals, progress, and benefits of the quantum-safe transformation. To maintain a sustained focus, provide consistent and robust updates on plans, transformation progress within the enterprise, advancements in quantum computing and their implications, and the efforts of others in the industry and ecosystem in their quantum-safe journeys.

- **Implement changes incrementally:** Implement changes incrementally to manage disruption and allow for adjustments based on feedback and observed issues. The iterative nature of this project provides plenty of opportunity to collect valuable feedback from users and factor it into subsequent iterations.

Vendor and Partner Alignment

We highlighted earlier that every enterprise depends on third-party software or service providers. Therefore, developing a deep understanding of the software supply chain for your enterprise is critical. Post-quantum cryptographic migration in the supply chain involves evaluating whether software vendors support cryptographic agility, whether their products are aligned with NIST-endorsed PQC algorithms, and whether they provide timely updates and roadmaps for quantum-safe readiness. Software bills of materials (SBOMs) can help identify cryptographic components and their transitive dependencies. As part of post-quantum cryptographic migration planning, enterprises should engage vendors with specific questions about PQC support, demand signed software updates, and update procurement policies to include quantum-safety criteria.

Ultimately, the integrity and security of the entire supply chain must be considered when transitioning to PQC. A failure in one component—such as a non-agile library or an insecure update mechanism—can undermine the security of the broader system, even if internal systems are fully migrated:

- **Collaborate with vendors:** Work closely with vendors and suppliers to ensure they are also transitioning to quantum-safe cryptography. Update your cryptographic inventory with the software and services provided by vendors. Note the PQC-ready software version that they will deliver and the date by which they will deliver them so that you can track their progress. Gather periodic updates from the vendors, and when they deliver PQC-ready software, insist that they provide an associated software bill of material (SBOM) and the cryptographic bill of materials (CBOM). Explore ways by which you can verify that the software delivered by them is indeed PQC compliant.

- **Align with partners:** Engage with business partners to align on quantum-safe strategies and ensure interoperability. Most, if not all, of the points mentioned for vendors apply to partners as well.

Collaboration and Community Engagement

Because every enterprise that exists must go through the transition to become quantum-safe, there are several industry groups and consortia that have been formed to collaborate and address the challenges of this large-scale transformation. It is important to be part of as many of these as needed so that you can learn from the collective experience of these communities. This is a very useful topic of discussion, and we cover this in more detail later in Chapter 7.

- **Participate in industry groups.** Engage with industry groups, standards bodies, and research communities focused on post-quantum cryptography.

- **Share insights.** Share findings, challenges, and successes with the broader community to contribute to the collective effort of achieving quantum-safe security.

Future-Proofing and Long-Term Strategy

Quantum computing has been evolving rapidly over the past few years and continues to accelerate its rate of progress. Quantum-safe solutions are advancing as well. NIST is already evaluating newer algorithms that will likely be added to the set already standardized. Standards bodies around the world are adapting their guidance based on NIST and other considerations. Regulatory, compliance, and governmental guidance are also emerging and are expected to gain momentum. The changes that are being made to migrate from classical cryptography to PQC must be future-proof, in that future changes need to be easily accommodated:

- **Plan for future developments.** Stay flexible and prepared for advancements in quantum computing and PQC. Crypto-agility is a vital component that enables this flexibility. More on this topic in the next chapter.

- **Perform regular reviews.** Given the rapid changes and evolution of guidelines, technologies, and so on, it is important that enterprises establish periodic reviews of the latest information and update their quantum-safe strategy to incorporate new developments, best practices, and insights.

Building the Roadmap

Having completed a business-driven risk assessment and a technology-based risk assessment and gained an understanding of business and technical dependencies, you are now ready to build your roadmap for quantum-safe transition that is specific to your enterprise using the guidance provided thus far on the various aspects to consider and include. As you can imagine, this will be developed as both incremental and iterative project initiatives. At the enterprise scale, very complex interdependencies need to be navigated. Consider using appropriate dependency management technologies to help catalog and visualize dependencies and support the creation of viable execution threads to maximize outcome and impact:

- **Organize project activities:** Robust orchestration of project activities must take into consideration business impact, risk, and dependencies of third-party and partner software services. The roadmap for execution must consider factors relevant to the enterprise to achieve the desired business objectives.

▪ **Update the roadmap periodically:** The success of the quantum-safe transition depends on having a robust and pragmatically executable roadmap. This roadmap depends on its ability to be dynamic to accommodate several key changes:

  ▪ Experiences from pilots, PoCs, and each phase of execution

  ▪ Advancements in capabilities from technology providers

  ▪ Experiences gained by integrators and best practices offered by consortia

  ▪ Organizational changes, priorities, and changes in the market landscape

Execution Approach

Several different best practices, approaches and actions regarding the journey to becoming quantum-safe have been mentioned thus far. What is important to bring out here is that the execution approach is not sequential or water fall like. Typically, there will be multiple parallel execution phases, and each phase will have many iterations. To illustrate this multi-pronged execution approach, we call out 3 phases.

Phase 1 is where we recommend addressing the following:

▪ Critical aspects of the IT infrastructure and applications that are identified to be higher risk

▪ Systems that have a higher potential of being a target for Harvest Now Decrypt Later attacks

▪ Systems that are dealing with sensitive data

▪ Applications that have to be addressed on account of regulatory compliance considerations, etc.

In this phase, approaches that enable accelerated quantum safe posture should be adopted, such as, deploying adaptive proxy-based solutions, upgrade of appropriate and, available PQC ready hardware or software, etc.

Phase 2, is where there is dependency on the software and hardware technology providers to upgrade their technology to be quantum-safe. Progress in this phase is likely to come in spurts as different vendors release at different times, quantum-safe versions of their libraries, software, etc. and, they in turn are adopted by enterprise applications and solutions. Enterprises need to monitor and manage these as informed by the business risk analysis compiled prior to execution.

Phase 3 focuses on enterprise IT systems that are entirely dependent on third-party product and application vendors for upgrades. Because these components fall outside the organization's direct control, tracking vendor readiness and product availability is crucial. In many cases, enterprises may discover that their operations rely heavily on such external products—yet have limited time to implement and thoroughly test critical changes once quantum-safe versions are released. Proactive preparation is essential: maintain an up-to-date inventory of vendor dependencies, develop contingency strategies, and have a detailed execution plan ready. This ensures the organization can act swiftly and effectively the moment quantum-safe versions of these third-party products become available.

Establish a Center of Excellence

The complex transition journey to becoming quantum safe must be guided and managed by a focused group of subject-matter experts (SMEs) and business and technology leaders within the enterprise. We call this group a *quantum-safe center of excellence (CoE)*. Establishing such a CoE and having its members engage in all the roadmap items described in this chapter is very important. This enables a core group of experts to emerge from within the organization to help guide the journey:

- **Engage a diverse group of individuals:** Identify disciplines (i.e., areas of expertise) that need to be covered as well as key roles that must be part of this CoE. Ensure that the skills and roles are augmented by external resources if such expertise is not available in the enterprise.

- **Establish stakeholder support:** Ensure that the CoE has support at the highest levels in the organization and becomes an execution arm that has visibility to the board of directors. The CoE should report progress at least quarterly to the board or the CEO.

Building a robust roadmap that is based on all the aspects discussed in this section and adopting a multi-pronged execution approach is a daunting task. This is where appropriate technology capabilities for codifying approaches, accelerating activities through tools, and automating the repeatable codified steps should be considered. At the time of writing this book, several robust tools are becoming available for various parts of this journey, but no silver bullet is available to address all the needs of an enterprise.

Pitfalls and Mitigation Strategies

The previous section highlighted many aspects that need to be taken into consideration while developing a post-quantum cryptographic migration strategy and roadmap as well as ultimately executing the roadmap to become quantum safe. We also mentioned using appropriate and available technology capabilities to assist and augment this journey. Because experience is the best way to deal with challenges, in this section we will share some pitfalls that we have seen enterprises encounter. We will then recommend appropriate strategies and approaches to prevent them (ideally) or to mitigate them if necessary.

Underestimating Complexity

At the expense of being redundant, we want to reiterate three main factors that contribute heavily to the contextual landscape:

- Cryptography and its dependencies are often deeply embedded within software components. These software components can be custom-developed by enterprises, procured from third-party vendors, or sourced from external ecosystem partners. Some of these are from embedded hardware IoT devices, HSMs, and so on.

- Most, if not all, enterprises do not have a current handle on their cryptographic posture: that is, what cryptography is used where, how, at what frequency, and covering what data.

- Finally, and perhaps most important, as we have said before, becoming quantum safe is a complex, multiyear journey, and almost every complex multiyear software transformation project results in cost and schedule overruns.

So, enterprises must be extremely careful not to underestimate the complexity of the effort.

One common mistake we have seen is that enterprises believe that the majority of, the source software and related software or infrastructure components they consume are provided by vendors, and therefore it is the responsibility of the vendors to provide the necessary PQC-updated software. When that happens, incrementally and over time, the enterprises will become quantum safe. This approach minimizes complexity and defers it entirely to providers. But keep in mind that a single failure in any of these individual components or their integration, or an omission in testing, could lead to potentially significant business risk and exposure, not to mention reputational risk.

A proven technique to deal with complexity is to break down the problem into smaller chunks. Business risk-based prioritization and dependency-driven use-case selection, as discussed earlier, will both help identify the executable scope of work. This, coupled with prudent selection of PoCs to test out approaches, selection of pilot projects to ensure that the right-sized use case is executed, and the codification of experiences as pattern-based learnings, will result in managing complexity effectively and gaining confidence and success in execution.

It is not our intent to overstate the challenges or seed fear, uncertainty, and doubt. But taking a pragmatic approach to develop a robust roadmap and a plan of execution that validates and verifies custom software and third-party components as and when they become available, and that proactively ensures that they will be available when needed, will be wise.

Insufficient Budget Allocation

Security-related initiatives that are not addressing an imminent threat are seldom prioritized and funded. Enterprises are becoming increasingly aware of the potential threat posed by future encryption compromises. Because the timing of this event is seemingly far in the future, allocation of sufficient funds to initiate the quantum-safe journey is still an issue. In addition, enterprise chief information security officers (CISOs) are often unable to estimate with supporting facts what overall budget is needed and over what period. As most boards of directors and CEOs expect a cost–benefit analysis of the investment ask, it is important to produce the business impact that may be caused by a threat that happens in the future. No practical models exist yet to address this challenge.

Some of the techniques and approaches that we have seen work well with enterprises are as follows:

- Continue to consistently educate key stakeholders about the advancements of quantum computing and guidelines proposed by governments, standards bodies, and regulatory authorities for the quantum-safe timeline. Key stakeholders must include the board of directors, CEO, CTO, CISO, and line-of-business executives who understand the business risk.

- Ask for a limited budget to develop a strategy, a set of PoCs, and pilots to get started. The outcome of this work should be a well-informed strategy and a clear plan to develop an execution roadmap. We have seen enterprises use this initial funding to inventory cryptography, analyze dependencies, identify crown jewels, and so on for a subset of their systems, and then use that information to develop a broader, enterprise-wide plan. This, when presented to the board, is seen as based on facts from within the enterprise's environment as opposed to a theoretical scenario.

- Leverage the expertise and experiences of technical business strategy consultants who have done this type of project before and can drive the development of a cost-benefit analysis based on the enterprise's data, and modeled information from peers in the industry. They can also leverage information being developed from within the industry consortia that may be applicable in this instance.

This is a problem faced by almost all enterprises, and with experience, some good models and approaches will emerge in the coming months or years. Staying connected with the industry organizations and peers in the ecosystem is a great way to tap into the latest updates.

Suboptimal Legacy System Remediation Approaches

Many enterprises have legacy systems that have been in production operation for dozens of years and often perform critical business functions, handling the "crown jewels" of the enterprise. These systems are highly sensitive and mission-critical, and in many cases, SMEs for these applications are hard to find or nearing retirement. Therefore, making these applications quantum safe becomes a very challenging task and typically falls into one of two approaches:

- Enterprises may leverage available SMEs to modify the software to make it quantum safe and at the same time introduce crypto-agility, such that future cryptography-related modifications can be made with minimal impact. This is clearly the desired approach for the long term and must be adopted wherever possible and where SMEs are available.

- In cases where SME availability is limited or nonexistent, judicious use of proxy-based solutions must be adopted. Adaptive proxy-based technologies are available that can be implemented in front of the legacy application, and all TLS connections to the application can be terminated there. To the various external services and applications connecting to the legacy application, this proxy will be the façade for the application. This proxy can adapt itself to communicate via classical, hybrid, or PQC-enabled protocols. This is a cost-effective solution that can be implemented where appropriate.

Enterprise must assess legacy systems with these approaches in mind and select and implement the right solution. This approach must be a key consideration as part of the end-to-end integration and testing strategy. It will result in a timely and risk-free implementation for making legacy applications quantum safe.

Crypto-agility as an Afterthought

Crypto-agility is a very important topic of consideration and discussion in the context of any enterprise's journey to become quantum safe. We have allocated a separate chapter to discuss crypto-agility in depth. However, we would be remiss if we did not highlight this as one of the often-ignored foundational architecture and design considerations:

- Crypto-agility must be a first-order consideration in planning the quantum-safe journey. When implemented as a foundational consideration, it is often observed that crypto-agility does not result in any added cost. In fact, the benefits of crypto-agile implementations far outweigh the perceived upfront cost of implementation.

- Retrofitting any system to be crypto agile requires much the same effort as implementing PQC in the first place. That is, technical debt is increased by not including crypto-agility.

- This may become a regulatory concern in the future. Although at the time of writing, no regulations require crypto-agility, discussions are underway to consider crypto-agility a requirement for certain industries.

More on this topic in Chapter 8.

Inadequate Preparation

There are several other areas that enterprises often do not adequately focus on. Although at first glance they may not seem important, neglecting them will prove to be as costly, if not more so, than the other pitfalls mentioned earlier. These points of omission result from the following mistakes:

- **Treating the PQC upgrade as a transactional one-time event:** Instead of looking at this migration as an evolution over time, if it is viewed as a one-time fix, then the first time a change needs to be made after the migration is complete, it will be expensive and will lead to recurring costs to fix things. The best way to avoid this is to build in cryptographic posture management or cryptographic life cycle management as part of the PQC transition. This is only minimally more expensive but will pay back the enterprise multiple times when future enhancements are needed or when managing cryptography on an ongoing basis.

- **Not selecting use cases appropriately:** Selecting the wrong use cases, not using appropriate risk-based prioritization for selecting use cases, and not understanding dependencies when selecting use cases all lead to wasted time and effort. The business objectives intended by the selected use cases will not be achieved or will yield minimal value. Selecting a use case that is too complex or too simple is equally suboptimal. The best way to avoid this is to use the approaches of business context-driven risk assessment, risk-based prioritization, and selection based on a deep understanding of dependencies.

- **Lack of focus on organizational change management and alignment:** As with any complex transformation project, ensuring that the right stakeholders are involved, engaged, and updated consistently on progress as well as challenges ensures that there are no surprises. This journey will involve challenges that the enterprise may not have faced before. Ensuring proper organizational support through these means is essential.

- **Not establishing clear metrics for success:** Breaking down the large scope of work into smaller building blocks is important. Equally important is establishing success measures for each of those building blocks and executing to accomplish them. These will help you discover what does and does not work, while also gaining experience that can be translated into best practices for the enterprise. Refactoring the roadmap from these learnings is the best way to make progress toward the goal.

Summary

An enterprise's successful quantum-safe transition is a complex transformation initiative that typically takes several years to complete. There are certain foundational principles that enterprises need to adhere to as they plan and execute this journey. Developing a sound strategy and preparing a pragmatic plan to execute it efficiently by leveraging all available guidance and best practices from the ecosystem is essential for success.

The creation of a robust roadmap is the lynchpin of this effort. Inventorying cryptographic artifacts, understanding dependencies, and adopting a business-led risk-based prioritization are essential in creating this robust roadmap.

There are various aspects to consider while creating an execution plan, and many of them are interconnected. An incremental and iterative approach that enables experience-based feedback to be factored into subsequent iterations has proven to be very productive and effective for most organizations.

Finally, do not let crypto-agility be an afterthought. It must be a first-order construct in the architecture, design, and execution of the quantum-safe journey.

References

(1) IBM, "Component business modeling: A private banking example," [Online]. Available: https://public.dhe.ibm.com/software/emea/dk/frontlines/IBM_BPM.pdf.

(2) IBM, "IBM Quantum-Safe Remediator Performance Harness," [Online]. Available: https://www.ibm.com/docs/en/quantum-safe/quantum-safe-remediator/1.1.0?topic=performance-harness.

(3) OQS, "OQS algorithm performance visualization," [Online]. Available: https://openquantumsafe.org/benchmarking.

Leveraging the Ecosystem

"Alone, we can do so little; together, we can do so much."

—Helen Keller

Very rarely do we see a scenario evolve that demands that every enterprise go through a very similar yet very significant transformation in a relatively short period of time. While this poses a significant challenge, it also presents a great opportunity to collaborate, learn from each other's experiences, and share learnings to help increase the rate of advancement. Becoming quantum-safe is one such transformation that requires every enterprise to complete the journey; therefore, leveraging the surrounding ecosystem is quite prudent and appropriate. This chapter calls out several collaborative entities that exist and raises awareness about the important work they do in addressing various aspects of the quantum-safe journey. While there are more consortia that exist than are mentioned here, enterprises should use this chapter as a guide to how they can collaborate with, contribute to, and learn from their peers in the industry, standards and regulatory bodies, and ecosystem-based consortia.

Collaboration with the Ecosystem

We have discussed in the previous chapter the importance of understanding the dependency of an enterprise across its ecosystem partners, vendors, and providers. Identifying these dependencies is itself an arduous task, let alone understanding and effectively managing them. This is where collaboration across the players in the industry ecosystem is critical. Becoming quantum safe can be thought of as a team sport. Enterprises must learn to effectively leverage the work being done in the industry by standards bodies, academia, industry organizations, partners, vendors, and even competitors. Several consortia exist, and we introduce many of them in this section.

National Cybersecurity Center of Excellence

The National Cybersecurity Center of Excellence (NCCoE) is a collaborative initiative led by NIST that brings together industry, government, and academic stakeholders to solve pressing cybersecurity challenges. Founded to accelerate the adoption of practical cybersecurity solutions, the NCCoE develops example implementations and practice guides that demonstrate how to apply standards-based approaches using commercially available technologies.

Its membership includes core collaborators who have signed Cooperative Research and Development Agreements (CRADAs) to provide expertise, technology, and necessary support. IBM, Cisco, AWS, Thales, Microsoft, and Splunk are some of the prominent collaborators. In addition, there are also collaborators provide project-specific guidance. Similarly, industry partners provide guidance on topics related to their specific industry.

A key strength of the NCCoE is its sector-specific approach, producing guidance tailored to industries such as finance, energy, healthcare, and manufacturing. The design points for their projects are that they need to be modular, repeatable, and scalable, helping organizations of all sizes adopt stronger security postures.

In the context of PQC, the NCCoE has launched initiatives to help enterprises understand, evaluate, and transition to quantum-resistant algorithms. Working closely with NIST's PQC standardization effort, the NCCoE provides guidance on cryptographic discovery, crypto-agility, and hybrid deployments, enabling organizations to prepare for quantum-enabled cybersecurity risks while maintaining interoperability.

By producing detailed NIST Cybersecurity Practice Guides (Special Publications 1800 series), the NCCoE empowers organizations with blueprints for secure implementations that address real-world challenges. Its open, collaborative model fosters innovation, accelerates best practices, and ensures that cybersecurity solutions are grounded in both technical excellence and operational relevance [1].

Post-Quantum Cryptography Coalition (PQCC)

The PQCC is a global initiative dedicated to preparing enterprises for their transition to quantum-safe cryptography. The PQCC aims to unite the public and private sectors to address the urgent need for post-quantum readiness by promoting collaboration, shared guidance, and coordinated action.

Founded with support from organizations such as the World Economic Forum and IBM, the PQCC includes a diverse membership of technology vendors, enterprise security leaders, academics, policymakers, and standards bodies. Its mission is to accelerate the adoption of PQC through education, best practices, community engagement, and implementation support.

The coalition plays a critical role in the following:

- Raising awareness about the quantum-enabled cybersecurity threats and "harvest now, decrypt later" (HNDL) risks

- Sharing practical migration strategies, including cryptographic inventory, agility, and hybrid deployments

- Engaging with regulators and standardization bodies, such as NIST, ETSI, and IETF, to align industry efforts with evolving guidance

- Fostering interoperability among vendors and solutions to avoid fragmentation in PQC adoption

The PQCC also encourages organizations to update procurement policies, product development lifecycles, and risk management frameworks to include quantum-safe requirements. It facilitates open collaboration and the exchange of technical and strategic insights through working groups, publications, and community events.

In a rapidly changing cryptographic landscape, the PQCC offers a vital platform for building shared knowledge, reducing migration friction, and ensuring a coordinated global response to the quantum threat [2].

Post-Quantum Cryptography Alliance (PQCA)

The PQCA is a collaborative initiative formed to accelerate the global transition to quantum-safe cryptography and build a secure digital future in the face of advancing quantum computing capabilities. It brings together a diverse ecosystem of stakeholders—including hardware vendors, software providers, cloud platforms, academic institutions, standards bodies, and enterprises—to coordinate efforts and reduce fragmentation across the cryptographic landscape.

The PQCA focuses on fostering the development, standardization, and deployment of post-quantum cryptographic technologies that can replace vulnerable classical algorithms such as RSA and ECC. Its core mission is to drive interoperability, support cryptographic agility, and ensure that post-quantum solutions are both technically sound and operationally practical for large-scale adoption.

One of the PQCA's strengths is its emphasis on open collaboration and vendor-neutral frameworks. It promotes the adoption of NIST-endorsed post-quantum algorithms, encourages the use of hybrid cryptographic models during the transition period, and supports the development of tools and libraries that ease integration into existing systems. The PQCA also contributes to technical working groups and standards bodies such as the IETF and ETSI, helping ensure alignment between research, implementation, and regulation.

By providing guidance on risk assessment, cryptographic inventory, migration roadmaps, and supply chain evaluation, the PQCA plays a key role in helping organizations prepare for and manage cryptographic modernization. It also advocates for crypto agile architectures and emphasizes the importance of education, policy alignment, and interoperable ecosystems. The PQCA serves as a critical global forum for aligning industry, academia, and government toward a secure, quantum-resilient future [3].

Although it may seem that these first three consortia are focused on the same areas, they have specific areas of focus and expertise and a necessary level of overlap to leverage each other's work. They share members, not just at the enterprise level, but also at the SME level. Their collective expertise and contributions are invaluable.

Post-Quantum Telco Network Task Force (PQTN)

The PQTN is a collaborative initiative launched in September 2022 by the Global System for Mobile Communication Association (GSMA), with founding members IBM and Vodafone, to address the impending security challenges posed by quantum computing to the telecommunications industry. This task force aims to define requirements, identify dependencies, and create a roadmap for implementing quantum-safe networking across global telecom infrastructures.

The PQTN focuses on facilitating the transition to PQC, ensuring that networks, devices, and systems are protected against future quantum threats. This includes addressing the HNDL risk.

The task force's work encompasses several key areas:

- **Cryptographic inventory:** Assessing existing cryptographic assets within telecom networks to identify vulnerabilities

- **Risk assessment:** Evaluating the potential impact of quantum threats on current systems and data

- **Migration strategies:** Developing plans to transition to PQC, including the adoption of hybrid models that combine classical and quantum-resistant algorithms

- **Standards alignment:** Collaborating with standardization bodies, such as NIST, ETSI, and IETF, to ensure consistency and interoperability in PQC adoption

- **Stakeholder engagement:** Involving a broad range of participants, including telecom operators, infrastructure providers, device manufacturers, and regulators, to foster a unified approach to quantum readiness

One of the task force's significant contributions is the publication of the PQ.1 Impact Assessment Whitepaper, which provides a comprehensive analysis of the challenges and recommendations for the telecom industry's transition to quantum-safe technologies. By proactively addressing quantum-enabled cybersecurity risks, the PQTN aims to safeguard the integrity and confidentiality of telecommunications, ensuring that the industry remains resilient in the face of emerging technological advancements.

This workgroup has been a forerunner and a poster child for other consortia workgroups. Members of this workgroup are invited to participate in other consortia and governmental workgroups and discussions to share their experience. Given that telecommunications is the foundation for all enterprise connectivity and global communication worldwide, the world is watching the progress and contributions of the PQTN [4].

Emerging Payments Association Asia (EPAA) Workgroup on Quantum-Safe Cryptography (WG-QSC)

The EPAA established the WG-QSC to proactively address the cybersecurity challenges posed by quantum computing within the payments industry. Launched at Money20/20 Asia in Bangkok in April 2024, the WG-QSC brings together leading financial and technology organizations, including Australian Payments Plus (AP+), HSBC, IBM, and PayPal as founding members.

The primary objective of the WG-QSC is to develop strategies for implementing PQC to safeguard payment infrastructures against the potential threats of quantum computers, to current encryption standards like RSA. The group focuses on several key areas:

- **Policy and regulation:** Analyzing existing frameworks to recommend updates that support the adoption of PQC

- **Business processes:** Assessing and redesigning operational procedures to integrate quantum-safe practices

- **Technical roadmap:** Identifying dependencies and use cases to create a comprehensive plan for transitioning to quantum-safe networks

The collaborative efforts are focused on understanding and implementing post-quantum protocols, defining approaches to protect critical payments infrastructure, processes, customer data, and payment flows through agreed-on policies, enhancing resilience in future networks.

The WG-QSC began by increasing the awareness of its constituency by publishing a myth-buster blog about quantum-safe cryptography, which was very well received and resulted in increased inquiries and participation. It also published its initial findings ahead of the Sibos conference in October 2024, providing guidance for the industry on adopting quantum-safe technologies. This proactive approach underscores the EPAA's commitment to ensuring the security and integrity of payment systems in the evolving digital landscape [5].

Nacha Quantum Payments Project Team

Nacha (formerly known as the National Automated Clearing House Association) oversees the electronic payment system of the United States, which facilitates direct deposits, bill payments, bank-to-bank transfers, and so on. The Nacha Payments Innovation Alliance established the Quantum Payments Project Team to proactively address the challenges and opportunities that quantum computing presents to the payments industry. This initiative aims to educate stakeholders about the implications of quantum computing for payment systems and to develop strategies for transitioning to quantum-safe cryptographic solutions.

The project team focuses on several key objectives:

- **Education and awareness:** Providing resources and sessions to help industry participants understand quantum computing fundamentals and its potential impact on payment security
- **Risk assessment:** Evaluating current cryptographic methods used in payment systems and identifying vulnerabilities that quantum computing could exploit
- **Strategic planning:** Developing actionable plans for adopting PQC, including timelines and best practices for implementation

In November 2024, the team released a report titled An Introduction to Quantum Computing and Payments, which explores how quantum computing could affect the payments industry, highlighting both potential innovations and significant security threats. Additionally, the team has produced educational materials such as the Buzzcast episode Demystifying Quantum Payments, to further disseminate knowledge and foster industry-wide preparedness.

Through these efforts, the Nacha Payments Innovation Alliance's Quantum Payments Project Team plays a crucial role in guiding the payments industry toward a secure and quantum-resilient future [6].

Financial Services Information Sharing and Analysis Center (FS-ISAC)

The FS-ISAC plays a critical role in the quantum-safe journey of the global financial sector. As the world's leading cyber intelligence sharing organization for financial institutions, the FS-ISAC provides a trusted platform for collaboration, awareness, and threat mitigation. In the context of PQC, the FS-ISAC serves as a central hub for raising awareness about the risks that quantum computing poses to cryptographic systems and for guiding its members through the transition to quantum-resistant security.

One of the FS-ISAC's key contributions is its role in facilitating the exchange of information about emerging threats, technical standards, and migration strategies related to PQC. By connecting financial firms, regulators, technology providers, and standards bodies, the FS-ISAC helps ensure that the industry's response to quantum risk is coordinated and proactive, rather than fragmented and reactive. This includes circulating best practices on cryptographic inventory, crypto agility, and secure implementation of hybrid algorithms, which are essential steps in building resilience before quantum attacks become feasible.

Moreover, the FS-ISAC's convening power enables the creation of working groups and cross-sector dialogues to address industry-specific implementation challenges. For instance, its focus on shared services, such as payment systems and interbank messaging platforms, ensures that quantum-safe upgrades are synchronized across the ecosystem, minimizing disruption and maintaining interoperability.

By supporting timely education, strategic planning, and joint exercises related to quantum preparedness, the FS-ISAC empowers its members to stay ahead of regulatory expectations and technological shifts. In doing so, it not only strengthens individual firms but also enhances the collective cybersecurity posture of the global financial system in the quantum era.

Through its PQC Working Group, the FS-ISAC has produced a comprehensive suite of resources to guide financial institutions in preparing for a quantum-safe future. Key publications include the following:

- **Risk Model:** Developed in collaboration with Wells Fargo, this model assists organizations in evaluating the risks associated with cryptographically relevant quantum computers (CRQCs). It provides a framework for prioritizing remediation efforts based on potential impacts.

- **Future State:** This paper outlines a roadmap for the financial services industry to transition to PQC, emphasizing the need for strategic planning and coordination.

- **Preparing for a Post-Quantum World by Managing Cryptographic Risk:** This document offers guidance on assessing current cryptographic assets and implementing quantum-resistant measures proactively.

- **Building Cryptographic Agility in the Financial Sector:** This whitepaper emphasizes the importance of crypto agility, enabling institutions to adapt to new cryptographic standards with minimal disruption.

Additionally, the FS-ISAC has addressed sector-specific concerns, such as the impact of quantum computing on the payment card industry, providing tailored guidance to mitigate associated risks.

These resources, along with FS-ISAC's ongoing efforts, underscore the organization's commitment to enhancing the cybersecurity resilience of the financial sector in the face of emerging quantum threats [7].

Quantum-Safe Financial Forum (QSFF)

Established by Europol's European Cybercrime Centre (EC3) in 2024, the QSFF is a pivotal initiative aimed at guiding the financial sector through the transition to PQC. The QSFF serves as a collaborative platform for stakeholders to develop strategies ensuring the security and resilience of financial infrastructures.

Comprising experts from major EU, UK, and U.S. commercial and central banks, as well as financial service providers and associations, the QSFF's mission is to foster a coordinated approach to PQC adoption. Notable participants include Banco Santander, Barclays, BBVA, BNP Paribas, CaixaBank, Rabobank, Intesa Sanpaolo, Mastercard, and the European Banking Federation. The forum emphasizes knowledge sharing, best practices, and the development of a unified threat assessment to facilitate a smooth transition to quantum-safe technologies.

In its publication Quantum-Safe Financial Forum: A Call to Action, the QSFF highlights the urgency of addressing the HNDL threat. The report outlines key recommendations, including the following:

- Prioritizing the transition to quantum-safe cryptography to protect sensitive financial data

- Coordinating among stakeholders to ensure alignment on planning, roadmaps, and implementation strategies

- Identifying and mitigating vulnerabilities in current cryptographic standards susceptible to quantum attacks

The QSFF also underscores the importance of integrating quantum risk considerations into existing regulatory frameworks, such as the EU's Digital Operational Resilience Act (DORA), to enhance the sector's preparedness.

Through its collaborative efforts, the QSFF aims to equip the financial industry with the tools and knowledge necessary to navigate the complexities of PQC migration, ensuring the continued security and trustworthiness of financial systems in the quantum era [8].

Others

Several other initiatives have been launched worldwide. The rapid increase in the number of initiatives being launched and the rate at which these are gaining momentum further underscores the growing awareness and concern among enterprises to appropriately address the needs of a successful quantum-safe journey by collaboratively leveraging the collective insights of the community around them.

Project Leap was launched by the Bank for International Settlements (BIS) Innovation Hub's Eurosystem Centre in partnership with the Bank of France and Deutsche Bundesbank. It aims to prepare central banks and the global financial system for a transition to quantum-resistant encryption. The project's initial phase tested the implementation of post-quantum cryptographic protocols between two central banks, focusing on maintaining the confidentiality of messages using hybrid encryption modes. Future phases plan to involve additional central banks to explore more complex IT environments, contributing to the broader goal of quantum-proofing the financial system [9].

In France, the RESQUE (RÉSilience QUantiquE) consortium brings together six cybersecurity entities: Thales, The GreenBow, CryptoExperts, CryptoNext Security, ANSSI, and Inria. Funded by the French government and the European Union's Next Generation EU scheme, the consortium focuses on developing post-quantum cryptographic solutions to protect communications, infrastructure, and networks against future quantum attacks. Key projects include creating a hybrid post-quantum virtual private network (VPN) and a high-performance post-quantum Hardware Security Module (HSM) [10].

Global PQC Guidance

As quantum computing evolves from theoretical breakthrough to commercial reality, global governments are responding with urgency and clarity—establishing national-level mandates and roadmaps for PQC migration. Business and technology leaders must now view PQC not as a niche cryptographic upgrade but as a foundational pillar of digital trust and long-term resilience. This section distills official guidance from the United States, Canada, European Union, United Kingdom, Australia, and India—highlighting practical directives, timelines, and policy shifts that enterprises must align with as part of a coordinated global response to the quantum threat. In short, adherence to governmental guidance is fast becoming a strategic imperative for commercial enterprises, governmental agencies, and other institutions.

In this section, we will provide an overview of the various governmental guidance and mandates that have been implemented thus far. This is an area where more work is being done and updates to guidance, including newer guidance where needed, executive orders, and even legislation, are expected to emerge. We encourage enterprises to closely track this development, ensure compliance as necessary, and incorporate these updates into their journey to become quantum safe. This section is only a sampling of what some countries have done. There are many more that have published guidance and are actively pursuing actions.

United States: Whole-of-Government Quantum-Safe Mandate

On June 6, 2025, the United States reinforced its commitment to quantum resilience through an executive order mandating the immediate adoption of PQC across all federal agencies. This directive builds on the NIST-standardized PQC algorithms—Kyber for encryption and Dilithium for digital signatures—by requiring agencies to inventory their cryptographic assets, identify quantum vulnerabilities, and develop phased implementation plans. Agencies are instructed to prioritize critical systems and deliver migration roadmaps within 180 days, ensuring alignment with government-wide benchmarks issued by the Office of Management and Budget (OMB) and the Cybersecurity and Infrastructure Security Agency (CISA).

Notably, this policy does not stop at the public sector. It calls on technology vendors and critical infrastructure providers to embed PQC into their supply chains and software offerings. By framing PQC as a secure-by-design requirement and integrating quantum-safe expectations into procurement and regulatory frameworks, the U.S. government is catalyzing industry-wide transformation. This approach exemplifies a proactive, standards-led model that enterprises can emulate to prepare for global interoperability and compliance.

Canada: Structured Transition Across Critical Systems

Canada's Cyber Centre issued its PQC Migration Roadmap on June 23, 2025, setting clear milestones for government departments to transition from classical to quantum-resistant cryptography. The roadmap requires a full inventory of cryptographic assets and risk assessments by March 2026, with critical systems to be transitioned by 2031 and all remaining systems by 2035. It encourages phased adoption strategies through pilot projects, crypto-agile architectures, and hybrid deployments that combine classical and post-quantum algorithms during the transition period.

For businesses and technology leaders, Canada's roadmap offers a pragmatic governance model: cross-agency collaboration, centralized IT support via Shared Services Canada, and regulatory oversight through the Treasury Board. Emphasis is placed on secure procurement, lifecycle management, and proactive vendor engagement. These practices serve as a blueprint for organizations aiming to future-proof their infrastructures, maintain regulatory compliance, and sustain public trust in digital services.

European Union: Coordinated Cross-Border Action Plan

The European Union's coordinated implementation roadmap, released in June 2025, provides a strategic framework for Member States to collectively transition to PQC. It mandates that foundational activities—such as awareness campaigns, cryptographic asset inventories, and risk assessments—be completed by 2026. By 2030, all critical infrastructure across energy, transportation, healthcare, and telecommunications must be quantum-safe. Broader public-sector systems are expected to comply by 2035.

The roadmap underscores the need for regulatory alignment with the NIS2 Directive, Digital Operational Resilience Act (DORA), and sectoral policies. It also introduces a cross-border governance mechanism under the NIS Cooperation Group, facilitating knowledge-sharing and pilot programs across industries and countries. Enterprises operating within or across the EU must now embed crypto-agility and standards compliance into their IT modernization strategies. The guidance stresses vendor accountability, cryptographic lifecycle visibility, and collaboration with industry stakeholders to ensure scalable, interoperable, and secure post-quantum systems.

United Kingdom: Phased Migration for Operational Continuity

In March 2025, the UK's National Cyber Security Centre (NCSC) published its Post-Quantum Cryptography Roadmap, articulating a three-phase migration strategy. Phase 1 (through 2026) focuses on discovery and readiness—organizations must inventory cryptographic assets and engage vendors on PQC roadmaps. Phase 2 (2026–2029) encourages hybrid cryptographic implementations and pilot programs within regulated sectors. Phase 3 (2029–2035) aims for complete transition to quantum-safe systems across government and critical national infrastructure.

The UK roadmap emphasizes the adoption of FIPS 140-3 validated cryptographic modules, integration of PQC into enterprise security strategies, and minimal operational disruption through lifecycle-based upgrades. Business and technology leaders are urged to avoid disruptive rip-and-replace approaches and instead implement crypto-agility—modularizing cryptography to enable agile updates. With its focus on regulatory coordination, vendor accountability, and system interoperability, the UK model promotes a pragmatic and risk-managed pathway toward cryptographic modernization.

Australia: Strategic Guidance via the ISM

Australia's 2025 update to its Information Security Manual (ISM) emphasizes the looming threat of quantum computing to public-key cryptography and provides actionable guidance for the public and private sectors. While not yet prescriptive in mandating PQC adoption, the ISM strongly recommends beginning the transition through hybrid models, crypto discovery, and system-wide cryptographic risk assessments.

Organizations are advised to prioritize cryptographic agility in future system designs and engage vendors to ensure PQC readiness in product roadmaps. The ISM recognizes NIST-approved algorithms—Kyber, Dilithium, and SPHINCS+—as key standards to monitor and adopt when certified under global validation programs. Business leaders are encouraged to prepare for quantum risk not only as a technical concern but also as a long-term trust and compliance issue, impacting data privacy, supply chain integrity, and digital service continuity.

India: National Technical Roadmap Anchored in Indigenous Innovation

India's Telecommunications Engineering Centre (TEC) released a comprehensive technical report in January 2025 detailing the nation's approach to PQC migration. Focused on security sovereignty and standard alignment, the roadmap recommends prioritizing lattice-based and hash-based cryptographic algorithms, including Kyber, Dilithium, and SPHINCS+. It identifies HNDL threats as a pressing concern and advocates the use of hybrid cryptography to mitigate data-at-rest risks in critical sectors such as telecom, banking, and defense.

The report urges organizations to prepare migration assessments, modernize cryptographic APIs, and align with secure hardware modules capable of supporting PQC. It also highlights the importance of ecosystem readiness, recommending collaboration with academia, startups, and standards bodies to accelerate indigenous capabilities and ensure global interoperability. India's model blends strategic foresight with national resilience, positioning PQC as a foundational layer in its digital public infrastructure.

Summary

Quantum-safe transformation is a team sport. Leveraging the collective insights and experiences of ecosystem and industry consortia is the best way to ensure that your enterprise's execution plan incorporates the latest information, best practices, and guidance. Be aware of what various countries are providing as guidance and regulatory expectations in this space.

References

(1) NIST, National Cybersecurity Center of Excellence, `https://www.nccoe.nist.gov`.

(2) MITRE, Post-Quantum Cryptography Coalition Launches, `https://www.mitre.org/news-insights/news-release/post-quantum-cryptography-coalition-launches`.

(3) The Linux Foundation, Post-Quantum Cryptography Alliance, `https://pqca.org`.

(4) GSMA, Post Quantum Telco Network Task Force, `https://www.gsma.com/solutions-and-impact/technologies/security/post-quantum-telco-network-task-force`.

(5) EPAA, Emerging Payments Association Asia announces new workgroup, `https://emergingpaymentsasia.org/wp-content/uploads/2024/04/25-April-EPAA-Press-Release-WG-QSC.pdf`.

(6) Nacha, Alliance Project Teams, `https://www.nacha.org/content/alliance-project-teams`.

(7) FS-ISAC, `https://www.fsisac.com`.

(8) EUROPOL, Quantum Safe Financial Forum, `https://www.europol.europa.eu/about-europol.european-cybercrime-centre-ec3/qsff`.

(9) Project Leap: quantum-proofing the financial system, `https://www.bis.org/about/bisih/topics/cyber_security/leap.htm`.

(10) World Economic Forum, `https://www.weforum.org/stories/2024/01/navigating-quantum-shift-preparing-people-products-systems-quantum-resilience`.

Achieving Crypto-Agility: Future-Proofing Your Business

"In the world of cybersecurity, the only constant is change.
Agility isn't an option—it's a necessity."
—Kevin Mitnick

In an era defined by accelerating technological change and mounting cryptographic risks—especially in the face of quantum computing—crypto-agility has emerged as a strategic imperative. It is no longer sufficient for organizations to deploy strong encryption; they must also be able to swiftly update, adapt, and retire cryptographic assets in response to evolving threats, compliance mandates, and algorithmic advances [1]. This chapter presents a comprehensive framework for crypto-agility to operationalize it across technology, governance, and culture. Readers will explore how to embed agility into their cryptographic architecture, foster cross-functional collaboration, and adopt emerging cryptographic technologies with minimal disruption. Through practical strategies and real-world insights, this chapter empowers business and technology leaders to balance flexibility with resilience, sustain innovation, and future-proof their organizations against current and quantum-era threats.

Defining Crypto-Agility and the Essential Framework

Establishing an adaptable cryptographic environment begins with clearly defining both the process and the framework that enable agility at scale. This starts by identifying the core requirements for managing cryptographic change, spanning technology, governance, and operations [2]. A well-defined process outlines how cryptographic assets are discovered, inventoried, assessed, and transitioned, and the framework provides the structural foundation to support this lifecycle consistently across the organization. It ensures alignment between technical design and policy enforcement, allowing for updates and replacements with minimal disruption. The framework also formalizes roles, responsibilities, and decision-making paths, enabling teams to act quickly and confidently in response to evolving standards, threats, or regulatory shifts. By embedding adaptability into architecture and operations through a defined approach, organizations can ensure that cryptographic agility is not left to chance but becomes an intentional, repeatable, and sustainable capability, positioning them to respond to change proactively and securely.

What Is Crypto-Agility?

Crypto-agility is the organizational capability to rapidly detect, update, and manage cryptographic algorithms, protocols, and related infrastructure in response to evolving threats, standards, or vulnerabilities—without requiring code rewrites, system redesigns, or operational downtime [3]. It ensures cryptographic resilience by decoupling the application logic from the underlying cryptographic implementations, thereby enabling quick and seamless transitions to safer primitives, including post-quantum cryptography. Emerging quantum computing capabilities threaten to undermine today's cryptographic foundations. Organizations must prepare not just to replace vulnerable algorithms, but to adapt continuously and without disruption. This is the essence of crypto-agility.

What Does It Take to Achieve Crypto-Agility?

Crypto-agility is a multidimensional capability that spans governance, architecture, tooling, and operations. It cannot be achieved through ad hoc upgrades or one-off cryptographic transitions [4]. Rather, it requires an enterprise-wide transformation in how cryptographic systems are managed, treating cryptography as a dynamic and critical part of digital infrastructure. Organizations must establish a structured approach to visibility, control, and execution around their cryptographic footprint.

Achieving crypto-agility demands more than upgrading libraries or rotating certificates. It involves all of the following:

- **Organizational awareness**: Alignment of business and technical leaders on the urgency and scope of cryptographic risks

- **Asset discovery**: Visibility into all cryptographic assets across software, hardware, networks, and supply chains

- **Flexible architectures**: Systems designed with pluggable crypto modules and standards-based interfaces

- **Tooling automation**: Automated inventory, monitoring, remediation, and key lifecycle management

- **Governance and policy**: Defined roles, deprecation schedules, compliance mandates, and third-party accountability

These elements must be embedded into the technology, culture, and operations of an organization.

A Framework-Led Approach

To successfully embed crypto-agility into the fabric of the enterprise, organizations need a repeatable and scalable framework that aligns strategy, engineering, compliance, and operations [5]. A framework-led approach ensures that crypto-agility is not reactive, but proactive: anticipated, measurable, and governed. It enables enterprises to confidently navigate cryptographic transitions, such as the post-quantum shift, with clear ownership and operational clarity.

A crypto-agility framework provides a structured blueprint to guide strategy, execution, and governance. It ensures that efforts are consistent, repeatable, and measurable.

The five core elements of this crypto-agility framework (Figure 8-1) are as follows:

1. **Governance and policy alignment**
   This element establishes formal governance structures, cryptographic ownership, and accountability mechanisms across the enterprise. It ensures that cryptographic policies are aligned with

organizational risk posture, regulatory obligations, and business priorities. Through defined roles, risk thresholds, escalation paths, and approval workflows, it enables coordinated decision-making and embeds cryptographic agility into broader cybersecurity and compliance frameworks.

2. **Modular cryptographic architecture**
   A modular architecture decouples cryptographic functions from business logic, applications, and infrastructure layers. It allows algorithms, protocols, and libraries to be replaced or upgraded without code-level disruption. This abstraction enables dynamic adaptability, supports hybrid cryptography, and simplifies transitions to post-quantum cryptography by ensuring that cryptographic changes can be implemented uniformly across heterogeneous environments.

3. **Adaptive protocol support**
   Adaptive protocol support provides flexibility to run multiple cryptographic protocols concurrently, allowing seamless coexistence of legacy, transitional, and quantum-safe algorithms. It enables selective protocol negotiation, dual encryption (hybrid modes), and policy-driven fallback mechanisms. This facilitates smooth migration, interoperability across systems, and a phased approach to cryptographic modernization without breaking dependencies.

4. **Operational tooling and technology automation**
   Automation accelerates and strengthens crypto-agility by integrating cryptographic asset discovery, usage classification, algorithm mapping, and remediation workflows into DevSecOps and runtime environments. AI-driven tools reduce manual effort, minimize misconfigurations, and improve response time. Automated testing, deployment, and rollback capabilities help maintain cryptographic integrity across development, deployment, and operational lifecycles.

5. **Continuous lifecycle management**
   Cryptographic assets require continuous oversight from provisioning to deprecation. This element involves maintaining accurate inventories, tracking usage, enforcing expiration and rotation schedules, and identifying weak or non-compliant cryptography. Lifecycle policies ensure that cryptographic materials remain current, aligned with evolving standards, and resilient against emerging threats through ongoing audits, rotation, and remediation.

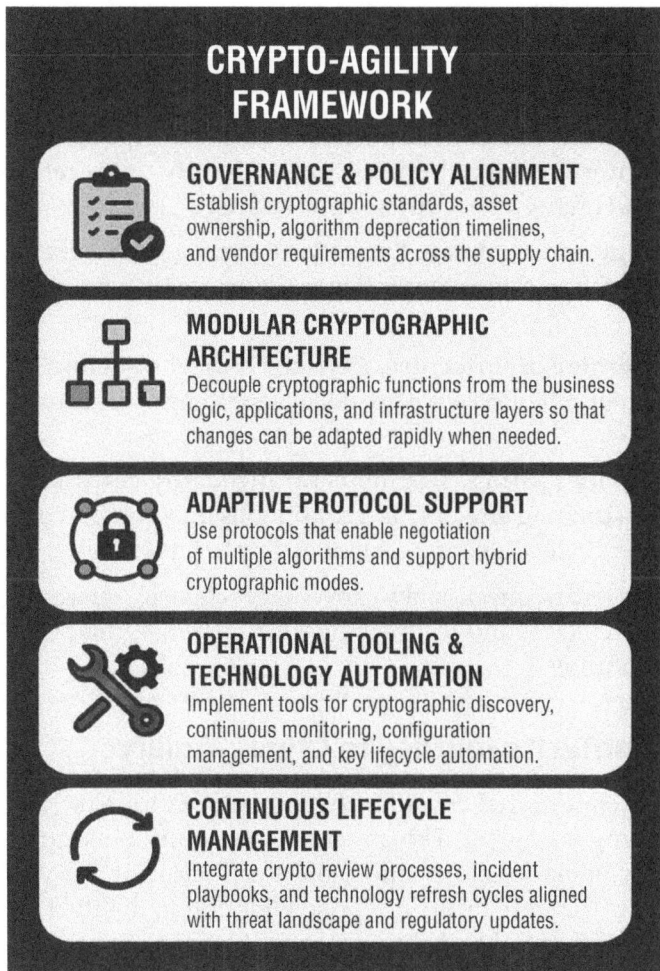

CRYPTO-AGILITY FRAMEWORK

GOVERNANCE & POLICY ALIGNMENT
Establish cryptographic standards, asset ownership, algorithm deprecation timelines, and vendor requirements across the supply chain.

MODULAR CRYPTOGRAPHIC ARCHITECTURE
Decouple cryptographic functions from the business logic, applications, and infrastructure layers so that changes can be adapted rapidly when needed.

ADAPTIVE PROTOCOL SUPPORT
Use protocols that enable negotiation of multiple algorithms and support hybrid cryptographic modes.

OPERATIONAL TOOLING & TECHNOLOGY AUTOMATION
Implement tools for cryptographic discovery, continuous monitoring, configuration management, and key lifecycle automation.

CONTINUOUS LIFECYCLE MANAGEMENT
Integrate crypto review processes, incident playbooks, and technology refresh cycles aligned with threat landscape and regulatory updates.

Figure 8-1: Crypto-agility framework

Implementing the Crypto-Agility Framework

Once the crypto-agility framework is defined, the next step is execution: turning strategy into practice. This involves mobilizing teams, integrating technologies, and setting up governance workflows [6]. The implementation must address current cryptographic exposure while future-proofing systems to accommodate emerging algorithms and policies. Each phase of implementation should be structured to yield measurable progress, reduce risk, and enhance system resilience.

The steps to lead crypto-agility at scale are as follows:

- **Step 1: Baseline assessment.** Conduct an enterprise-wide cryptographic inventory using automated tools. Identify deprecated algorithms and high-value cryptographic assets.

- **Step 2: Strategy and roadmap.** Define your crypto-agility goals, timelines, and risk prioritization strategy. Allocate cross-functional roles.

- **Step 3: Modernize architecture.** Refactor critical systems for modular cryptography. Replace hardcoded algorithms with abstract interfaces.

- **Step 4: Integrate tooling.** Deploy centralized key/certificate management, scanning engines, and continuous integration/continuous delivery (CI/CD) enforcement of crypto policies.

- **Step 5: Govern and iterate.** Establish governance councils, quarterly crypto health reviews, and technology pilots for emerging post-quantum algorithms.

Case Study: OrionTech's Journey to Crypto-Agility

To bring the framework to life, consider the journey of OrionTech, a global digital banking leader [7]. This practical case study illustrates how strategic vision, operational execution, and a commitment to cryptographic resilience can culminate in enterprise-wide crypto-agility. The company's experience highlights the importance of leadership buy-in, tooling integration, protocol modernization, and cultural transformation.

Company overview: OrionTech relied heavily on Rivest-Shamir-Adleman (RSA) and elliptic curve cryptography (ECC) for data protection. With increasing threats of quantum compromise, the company embarked on a crypto-agility transformation.

The timeline of activities was as follows:

1. **Governance**: Created a cryptographic governance task force. Issued policies for deprecated algorithms and vendor compliance.

2. **Inventory**: Used Cryptographic Bill of Materials (CBOM) scanners across 2,000+ applications. Mapped crypto use to business-critical workflows.

3. **Architecture overhaul**: Refactored key systems to use crypto-abstraction libraries.

4. **Protocol upgrade**: Transitioned to Transport Layer Security (TLS) 1.3 hybrid key exchange with post-quantum cryptography (PQC) candidates (Kyber + ECC).

5. **Tooling**: Integrated certificate lifecycle automation and telemetry dashboards.

6. **Full rollout**: Executed phased migration with rollback controls. Post-migration audit confirmed 90% hybrid adoption.

7. **Sustainability**: Instituted a crypto review board and lab pilots for Falcon and Dilithium.

Outcome: OrionTech achieved quantum-safe readiness in 24 months without a service disruption. Security ratings improved, and the firm set new procurement standards for third-party software crypto hygiene.

Cultivating a Culture of Crypto-Agility Across the Organization

In an era defined by rapid cryptographic evolution and quantum threats on the horizon, technology alone is not enough [8]. Organizations must cultivate a **culture of crypto-agility**: a strategic posture that enables them to adapt cryptographic protections with speed, coordination, and confidence. This transformation is not confined to IT or security teams. It spans every function, from executive leadership to development, procurement, compliance, and beyond.

At its essence, cultivating crypto-agility means embedding cryptographic responsiveness into everyday decisions. It is the shift from reactive encryption patching to proactive cryptographic resilience. And it begins with people and process, not just products.

Executive Leadership and Risk Ownership

Crypto-agility starts at the top. Executive support is the engine of cultural transformation [9]. Leaders must treat cryptographic risk not as a niche technical concern but as a board-level issue on par with financial, operational, and reputational risks. Elevating cryptographic health to the enterprise risk register signals its significance across the organization.

CISOs, CTOs, and Chief Risk Officers should be explicitly accountable for crypto-agility initiatives. Some organizations go further by establishing dedicated **cryptographic governance committees** or appointing a **Head of Cryptography Strategy**: a cross-functional leader who drives alignment across engineering, compliance, and procurement.

Example: A global telecom enterprise launched a quarterly Crypto Resilience Report for its board. This executive dashboard tracked cryptographic inventory health, quantum-readiness status, and risk mitigation progress. It helped secure additional investment for crypto-modernization and led to the appointment of a cryptography strategy lead reporting to the CTO.

These are the strategic recommendations:

- Add cryptographic threats to enterprise risk frameworks.
- Include crypto-resilience in cybersecurity board presentations.
- Designate executive accountability for crypto-agility programs.

Enterprise-Wide Training and Awareness

Cryptography can often feel abstract or inaccessible to non-experts. That's why culture change begins with education [10]. Crypto-agility thrives when everyone—from developers to legal teams—has the right level of understanding.

Training should be tiered and role-specific, as described in Figure 8-2. Executives need business context and impact. Legal and compliance teams need to understand regulatory implications. Developers require hands-on knowledge of APIs, standards, and secure design patterns. DevSecOps teams must be trained to respond to algorithm deprecation and incorporate cryptographic updates into CI/CD pipelines.

The key tactics for the success of driving crypto-awareness are as follows:

- Embed cryptography modules in employee onboarding.
- Host "Crypto Days" with internal experts and guest speakers.
- Launch just-in-time training for algorithm transition cycles.
- Use gamified threat simulations to boost engagement.

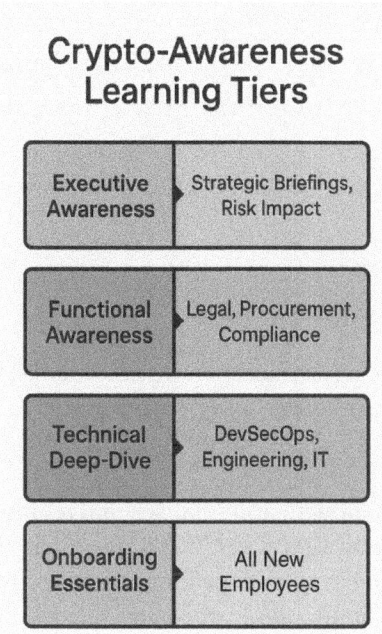

Figure 8-2: Crypto-awareness learning tiers

Secure Development Practices

Developers are on the frontlines of crypto-agility. Yet too often, cryptographic decisions are hardcoded into applications, making updates complex and risky. The path forward lies in modularity, standardization, and continuous integration.

By abstracting cryptographic choices through centralized software development kits (SDKs), APIs, or policy engines, organizations gain the flexibility to switch algorithms or update configurations without rewriting business logic. Integrating cryptographic checks into the secure software development lifecycle (SSDLC) ensures consistency from design to deployment.

Example: A leading fintech company adopted a centralized cryptographic SDK that enforced enterprise policy. When migrating to hybrid post-quantum cryptography, developers didn't change a single line of application code—only the backend configuration was updated.

These are the developer enablement strategies:

- Adopt approved cryptographic libraries with abstraction layers.
- Provide secure architecture blueprints and reference implementations.
- Integrate crypto-validation tools in CI/CD workflows.
- Conduct periodic cryptographic code audits.

Vendor and Procurement Alignment

An organization's cryptographic posture doesn't end at its perimeter [11]. SaaS providers, supply chain partners, and third-party platforms can all introduce hidden cryptographic risks. Thus, procurement and vendor management functions must evolve.

As shown in Figure 8-3, contracts must now include clauses that require cryptographic transparency, algorithm agility, and CBOM disclosures. Vendor risk assessments should examine cryptographic configurations, algorithm lifecycle policies, and key management processes.

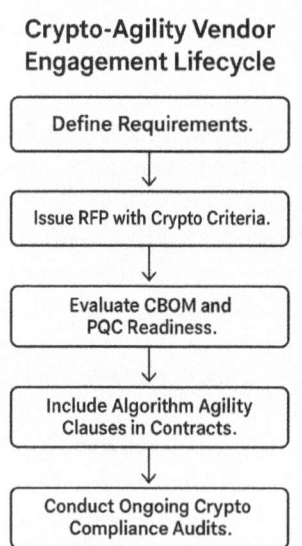

Figure 8-3: Crypto-agility vendor engagement lifecycle

Here are the procurement practices to adopt:

■ Standardize CBOM requirements in all security questionnaires.

■ Prioritize vendors supporting post-quantum cryptographic agility.

■ Define clear service-level agreements (SLAs) for crypto updates and transparency.

■ Include cryptographic audits in regular vendor assessments.

Continuous Measurement and Improvement

Crypto-agility is not a one-time project. It's a living discipline that requires continual tuning [12]. Organizations must define key performance indicators (KPIs) that reflect both compliance and readiness. Examples include the following:

■ Percentage of systems using NIST-approved algorithms

■ Time to remediate deprecated crypto usage

■ Key rotation frequency across systems

■ CBOM compliance across vendors

These metrics should feed into crypto posture dashboards reviewed at regular security councils or business unit meetings.

Example: An international energy firm implemented a Crypto-Agility Index combining algorithm coverage, key lifecycle health, and vendor compliance. This score informed quarterly executive reviews and directly influenced funding allocations for security modernization.

Use these feedback and evolution tactics:

■ Run annual red-team assessments on cryptographic systems.

■ Monitor National Institute of Standards and Technology (NIST) and industry algorithm updates and advisories.

■ Conduct post-incident reviews with cryptographic lessons learned.

■ Establish an internal crypto-champions community of practice.

Creating a culture of crypto-agility is not about turning every employee into a cryptographer. It's about building awareness, accountability, and adaptability into the organizational DNA. It ensures that when cryptographic change is necessary—whether due to quantum risk, regulatory shifts, or algorithm compromise—the enterprise can respond with clarity, speed, and control.

Three pragmatic approaches allow enterprises to future-proof their cryptographic systems efficiently even in complex or resource-constrained environments: cryptographic abstraction; transparent cryptographic gateways; and automated cryptographic discovery, risk assessment, and remediation.

Leveraging Cryptographic Abstraction and Centralization

The first strategy centers on abstraction: decoupling cryptographic logic from application code. Enterprises should avoid embedding algorithm-specific code into applications and instead adopt centralized crypto-graphic services such as SDKs, APIs, or policy-driven encryption proxies. This approach allows developers to delegate cryptographic operations to a centralized authority that enforces standards and manages agility behind the scenes.

Such centralization simplifies the transition to new algorithms (e.g., quantum-safe hybrids) because the application itself doesn't need to change—only the configuration or backend library is updated. It also ensures consistent implementation, reduces errors, and improves audit-ability.

Example: A global payment provider adopted an internal cryptography-as-a-service platform. When NIST finalized its post-quantum candidates, only the service backend was updated to support hybrid key encapsulation mechanisms (KEMs). None of the customer-facing applications required modification.

Key benefits:

- No direct code refactoring required
- Supports rapid cryptographic updates via policy changes
- Enables consistent enterprise-wide cryptographic governance

Deploying Transparent Cryptographic Gateways

A powerful approach for organizations with large legacy estates is to use transparent cryptographic gateways or adaptive proxy layers. These solutions intercept data in transit or at rest and apply modern cryptographic transformations—without requiring changes to applications, data structures, or business workflows.

This is especially effective for third-party integrations or legacy systems that are too costly or risky to rewrite. Transparent proxies can be deployed inline or as part of the infrastructure (e.g., TLS termination points, secure reverse proxies, or storage adapters), enabling enterprises to upgrade their cryptographic posture with no service downtime.

Example: A regional bank deployed an adaptive TLS proxy that automatically negotiated post-quantum algorithms with external partners while maintaining legacy cipher suites internally. This allowed the firm to meet regulatory mandates without altering core banking systems.

Deployment use cases:

- Securing legacy applications from "harvest now and decrypt later" (HNDL) attacks
- Providing post-quantum encryption to data lakes and backups
- Layering over Internet of Things (IoT) and edge devices with constrained firmware

Automating Discovery, Remediation, and Lifecycle Management

Cryptographic agility also depends on visibility and automation. Many enterprises lack an accurate inventory of cryptographic assets: algorithms, keys, certificates, and protocols in use. This invisibility creates operational friction when updates are required. Automating cryptographic discovery, risk assessment, and remediation workflows can eliminate manual overhead and accelerate compliance with emerging standards.

Leading organizations are deploying cryptographic posture management (CPM) platforms that continuously scan environments (applications, databases, network flows, certificates), classify assets, and flag deprecated algorithms or configurations. These tools also integrate with CI/CD pipelines and IT service management (ITSM) systems, enabling policy-driven remediation without developer or operator involvement.

Example: A major healthcare provider implemented a crypto-inventory and risk dashboard. Within 90 days, it discovered 1,200 instances of outdated SHA-1 certificates and automated their replacement using integrated certificate lifecycle management—improving security while reducing manual effort by 70%.

Operational efficiencies:

- Zero-touch remediation of expired or insecure crypto assets
- Continuous risk scoring aligned with business impact
- Integration with existing security operations and compliance systems

Enterprises no longer need to choose between security and simplicity. With cryptographic abstraction, transparent proxies, and automation platforms, organizations can achieve agile adoption of quantum-safe and next-generation cryptographic technologies without disrupting business operations or draining technical resources.

This shift is not just a technical transition but a strategic evolution. Crypto-agility becomes a force multiplier: enabling compliance, reducing risk, and positioning the enterprise for resilient growth in a post-quantum world.

Balancing Security and Flexibility in a Crypto-Agile Environment

Crypto-agility is not just a technical necessity; it is a delicate balancing act between uncompromising security and enterprise-grade flexibility. Business and technology leaders must ensure that this flexibility does not open the door to governance failures, misconfigurations, or regulatory risks. This section presents a structured guide to achieving that balance.

Understanding the Dual Mandate: Security and Flexibility

In designing for crypto-agility, many organizations risk over-prioritizing speed and flexibility, potentially bypassing critical controls. Here are some examples:

- Allowing unaudited dynamic changes to crypto settings in applications
- Permitting hybrid configurations (e.g., RSA + PQC) without strict policy enforcement
- Skipping validation during rapid library upgrades

Without structured controls, agility can become a liability.

Therefore, business leaders must frame crypto-agility as a controlled flexibility: a capability that empowers adaptation but within a governed, policy-driven, secure framework.

Building a Secure Yet Agile Cryptographic Architecture

Building a secure yet agile cryptographic architecture requires balancing strong encryption with flexibility. By designing modular, interoperable systems that support seamless updates, organizations can adapt to evolving threats and standards without disruption. This approach ensures long-term resilience, operational continuity, and readiness for post-quantum and regulatory-driven cryptographic changes.

Key Principles for Security-First Agility

Balancing security and flexibility starts with architecture. Secure-by-design principles must be embedded into cryptographic agility workflows and infrastructure.

Modularity and Abstraction

Design cryptographic interfaces (e.g., APIs) to abstract away algorithms and libraries. Applications should not be tightly coupled to specific ciphers or providers. This ensures seamless algorithm swaps and future-readiness.

Centralized Cryptographic Posture Management (CPM)

Maintain a **centralized inventory** of all cryptographic assets—keys, certificates, protocols, and algorithms. This real-time visibility allows security teams to detect outdated or non-compliant components.

Policy Automation

Leverage **policy-as-code** to define which algorithms are allowed, required, or deprecated. Enforce these policies across CI/CD pipelines, runtime environments, and developer workspaces.

Role-Based Controls and Governance

Introduce strict access management for cryptographic modifications. Not all DevOps teams should have rights to alter cryptographic libraries or key configurations. Ensure governance through role-based access control (RBAC), audits, and logs.

Guardrails for Flexibility

Modularity empowers change, but it must be supported with the following:

- **Automated testing** of cryptographic changes during build and release cycles
- **Interoperability validation**, especially in hybrid algorithm deployments (e.g., TLS with Dilithium + ECC)
- **Change review boards**, including security leads, for approving crypto configuration changes in production systems

By embedding these controls, organizations ensure that flexibility never comes at the cost of confidentiality, integrity, or compliance.

Operationalizing Crypto-Agility at Scale

Operationalizing crypto-agility at scale involves embedding automation, policy enforcement, and continuous monitoring across enterprise systems. It ensures rapid cryptographic updates, streamlined key and certificate management, and integration with DevSecOps pipelines. This scalable approach enables organizations to respond swiftly to threats, compliance shifts, and algorithm changes with minimal disruption.

Enablers of Agile and Secure Operations

Enablers of agile and secure operations include modular cryptographic architectures, automated key lifecycle tools, real-time posture monitoring, and policy-driven governance. These elements work together to support seamless cryptographic transitions, reduce manual overhead, and ensure compliance. They form the foundation for resilient, responsive, and secure cryptographic environments across dynamic digital ecosystems [13].

Hybrid Cryptography for Transition

Adopt hybrid cryptographic models that pair PQC with classical algorithms (e.g., X25519 + Kyber). These offer forward-compatibility while ensuring backward support with existing systems.

Crypto Lifecycle Automation

Implement certificate lifecycle management (CLM), key rotation scheduling, and algorithm rollout using automated orchestration tools. Manual intervention in cryptographic updates increases both delay and risk.

DevSecOps Integration

Embed crypto-agility into DevSecOps pipelines through the following:

- Automated scans of source code and builds for insecure or outdated algorithms
- Gatekeeping policies that prevent code pushes containing noncompliant crypto
- Security playbooks for approved PQC migration paths

Cross-Functional Collaboration

Crypto-agility is not the sole responsibility of security teams. Legal, compliance, software engineering, IT operations, and risk officers must co-own the strategy. Business units should be briefed on crypto risks and how agility aligns with customer trust and market reputation.

Continuous Monitoring and Threat Intelligence

Quantum threats are evolving. SIEM and threat intel platforms must include **quantum-aware indicators** such as PQC vulnerability scans, NIST PQC finalist adoption progress, and vendor library deprecations.

Agility without control is chaos. Security without agility is stagnation. The key is to architect and operationalize cryptographic systems that are flexible yet governed—modular yet monitored—dynamic yet secure.

Business and technology leaders must do the following:

- Define crypto-agility as a strategic objective.

- Invest in secure-by-design architectures.

- Embed automation, monitoring, and cross-functional governance.

Only then can organizations truly balance security and flexibility in a way that supports resilience, innovation, and long-term trust.

Sustaining Crypto-Agility: Continuous Improvement and Innovation

As enterprises begin adapting to a quantum-threatened digital future, crypto-agility—the ability to adapt cryptographic systems without disruption—has become an organizational necessity. Yet achieving crypto-agility is not a one-time milestone. It requires ongoing vigilance, investment, and innovation. Enterprises must treat crypto-agility as a living capability, evolving continuously through improvements in policy, architecture, process, and tooling.

The following three steps guide business and technology leaders on how to sustain crypto-agility with a structured approach to continuous improvement, operational discipline, and innovation leadership.

Strategic Foundations: Embedding Agility into the Enterprise DNA

Crypto-agility must evolve from a reactive initiative to a strategic security posture. This transformation begins at the leadership level, with mindset, ownership, and investment.

Aligning Agility to Business Risk

Executives must clearly understand and communicate why crypto-agility is essential not only to meet post-quantum cryptographic standards but also to:

- Mitigate evolving threats (e.g., cryptographic zero-days, PQC breakthroughs)
- Maintain customer trust in secure services

- Accelerate regulatory response (e.g., to NIST or GDPR-aligned crypto mandates)

- Ensure mergers and acquisitions (M&A) agility, especially when integrating systems with varied crypto implementations

Aligning crypto-agility with board-level risk management helps secure long-term funding and support for sustaining investments.

Enterprise-Wide Policy Anchoring

Crypto-agility must be codified through policy:

- Mandate cryptographic lifecycle governance.

- Define agility-specific KPIs (e.g., time to patch crypto libraries, algorithm migration lead times).

- Establish escalation paths for cryptographic incidents (e.g., compromised algorithms, deprecated libraries).

Leaders should position crypto-agility as a cross-cutting principle that is embedded into data protection, application security, CI/CD pipelines, and incident response.

Operational Execution: Driving Continuous Improvement at Scale

To sustain agility, enterprises must establish repeatable, measurable, and evolving processes. This enables not just readiness, but adaptability.

Cryptographic Posture Management (CPM)

Maintain a live inventory of cryptographic assets—including certificates, keys, libraries, APIs, and protocols—across hybrid environments. Use CPM tools that do the following:

- Continuously scan for outdated, noncompliant, or deprecated algorithms

- Automate remediation workflows

- Support hybrid and PQC transition paths

Regular posture reviews ensure that the organization keeps up with emerging crypto standards and vulnerabilities.

Policy-Driven Automation

Manual cryptographic upgrades are error-prone and slow. Sustained agility requires automation:

- Certificate lifecycle automation (issuance, rotation, revocation)
- Policy enforcement as code (e.g., minimum key sizes, approved algorithm lists)
- Cryptographic regression testing in CI/CD

Continuous improvement is enabled by feedback loops, where detection informs policy, and policy drives execution.

Metrics and Maturity Tracking

Establish a cryptographic agility maturity model, tracking the following:

- % of crypto assets under visibility
- Mean time to recovery (MTTR) for algorithm changes
- Coverage of PQC-readiness pilots across systems

These metrics serve as health indicators of agility. Leaders should review them quarterly, just as they would uptime, compliance, and threat metrics.

Innovation and Foresight: Sustaining Agility Through Research and Ecosystem Collaboration

Sustainability in crypto-agility also requires forward-looking investment in new technologies, standards, and collaborative ecosystems.

R&D and Pilot Programs

Quantum-safe cryptography is still evolving. Enterprises must do the following:

- Allocate R&D funds to evaluate PQC finalists and new hybrid schemes (e.g., Kyber, Dilithium, BIKE).
- Run pilot projects with controlled rollout in email, virtual private networks (VPN), TLS, and public-key infrastructure (PKI).
- Simulate HNDL attack resilience.

Experimentation must be governed but consistent. A culture of test-and-learn ensures readiness for rapid adoption of new standards.

Vendor and Industry Collaboration

Enterprises should actively engage with:

- Standards bodies like NIST, the European Telecommunications Standards Institute (ETSI), and the International Organization for Standardization (ISO) for PQC migration guidance
- Vendors for product PQC roadmaps and crypto-agile SDKs
- Peer groups such as the Financial Services Information Sharing and Analysis Center (FS-ISAC), Business Software Alliance (BSA), and the Quantum Economic Development Consortium (QED-C) for knowledge-sharing on crypto migration and threat modeling.

These collaborations yield early access to innovations, reference implementations, and risk intelligence.

Continuous Threat Intelligence and Adaptation

Agility must also account for threat dynamics. Maintain dedicated security functions that do the following:

- Track quantum research breakthroughs (e.g., qubit scaling, cryptoanalytic advances)
- Monitor deprecation timelines for classical algorithms (e.g., RSA, ECC)
- Analyze supply chain and vendor crypto readiness

This intelligence must feed both operational and strategic decision-making to ensure that crypto-agility evolves with the risk landscape.

Crypto-agility is not a box to check; it is a core security capability that must be renewed, refined, and reimagined over time. Business and technology leaders must take an architectural, operational, and strategic approach to sustaining it by:

- Embedding crypto-agility into enterprise strategy
- Driving operational excellence through policy and automation
- Leading innovation through foresight and collaboration

Organizations can ensure that crypto-agility remains a resilient foundation, ready for whatever cryptographic challenges the future may bring.

The result? A digitally trusted enterprise that can adapt rapidly to change, maintain compliance, and safeguard data integrity in a post-quantum world.

Summary

Crypto-agility is the cornerstone of future-ready cybersecurity and a critical enabler for business resilience. This chapter outlined how organizations can build crypto-agility through a framework-led approach that aligns governance, architecture, and operations. It emphasized cultivating an adaptive culture, adopting new cryptographic technologies with minimal disruption, and striking a balance between strong security and operational flexibility.

For business and technology leaders, the path to quantum-safe security begins with a proactive, well-governed cryptographic strategy. Sustaining crypto-agility requires continuous improvement, automation, and cross-functional collaboration. By embedding agility across the cryptographic lifecycle, organizations can confidently respond to evolving threats, regulatory changes, and technology shifts, ensuring long-term trust, compliance, and innovation.

References

(1) NIST cybersecurity white paper, "Considerations for Achieving Crypto Agility" (NIST.CSWP.39.ipd). https://csrc.nist.gov/pubs/cswp/39/considerations-for-achieving-cryptographic-agility/2pd.

(2) NIST SP 800-208: Recommendation for Stateful Hash-Based Signatures. https://csrc.nist.gov/publications/detail/sp/800-208/final.

(3) NIST SP 800-175B: Guideline for Using Cryptographic Standards. https://csrc.nist.gov/publications/detail/sp/800-175b/rev-1/final.

(4) NIST Post-Quantum Cryptography Standardization Project. `https://csrc.nist.gov/projects/post-quantum-cryptography`.

(5) ISO/IEC 19790:2025, Security Requirements for Cryptographic Modules. `https://www.iso.org/standard/82423.html`.

(6) U.S. Department of Homeland Security, Post-Quantum Cryptography Guidelines. `https://www.dhs.gov/quantum`.

(7) World Economic Forum, Quantum Computing Governance Principles. `https://www.weforum.org/reports/quantum-computing-governance-principles`.

(8) IBM Quantum Safe Overview and Industry Practices. `https://www.ibm.com/quantum/quantum-safe`.

(9) ISACA, Post-Quantum Cryptography Preparedness 101. `https://www.isaca.org/resources/news-and-trends/isaca-now-blog/2024/post-quantum-cryptography-preparedness-101`.

(10) NSA Commercial National Security Algorithm Suite 2.0. `https://media.defense.gov/2025/May/30/2003728741/-1/-1/0/CSA_CNSA_2.0_ALGORITHMS.PDF`.

(11) Gartner, Data and Analytics Leaders Primer for 2022. `https://www.gartner.com/en/documents/4010123`.

(12) ETSI Quantum-Safe Cryptography Standards. `https://www.etsi.org/technologies/quantum-safe-cryptography`.

(13) World Economic Forum – Real World Cryptographic Agility. `https://initiatives.weforum.org/quantum/case-study-details/real-world-cryptographic-agility/aJYTG0000000KWb4AM`.

A Vision of Securing the Digital World in the Quantum Era

"I never think about the future. It comes soon enough."

—Albert Einstein

As quantum computing rapidly advances from theoretical promise to practical reality, the implications for cybersecurity are profound and immediate. This chapter serves as a forward-looking synthesis of this book's core message: ushering enterprises toward a resilient, quantum-safe future.

Here we explore how quantum-safe principles intersect with the digital innovations defining the next decade: artificial intelligence, augmented and virtual reality, cloud and hybrid computing, edge intelligence, 5G/6G networks, the Internet of Things (IoT), zero trust frameworks, blockchain ecosystems, software-defined infrastructure, and quantum computing itself. Each of these technologies depends on cryptographic trust, and each faces disruption from quantum-computing-based opportunities. Rather than viewing cryptographic transformation as a narrow IT concern, this chapter positions it as a boardroom-level imperative, touching every layer of digital infrastructure and every corner of enterprise innovation. Business and technology leaders must understand that the convergence of quantum risk with emerging tech creates both vulnerability and opportunity.

Done right, becoming quantum safe is not just about defense: it's a strategic investment in trust, agility, and future leadership that could very well be a differentiator. We discuss actionable insights and guidance to embed post-quantum security across these interconnected domains, empowering leaders to navigate uncertainty with confidence and build organizations that are not just digitally transformed but cryptographically future-proof.

Looking Ahead to a Quantum-Safe World

Quantum computing is no longer a distant possibility—it's an imminent reality. Its transformative power poses a direct challenge to the cryptographic systems that secure our digital world. From safeguarding sensitive data to protecting critical infrastructure, the foundations of digital trust are at risk. For business and technology leaders, the message is unmistakable: the question is no longer if quantum computing will break today's asymmetric cryptography—it's when [1]. Preparation must begin now [2].

Throughout this book, we've examined the scope of quantum threats, the vulnerabilities they expose, and the technologies and frameworks designed to defend against them. But becoming quantum safe isn't just about swapping algorithms. It requires a shift in how organizations treat cryptography: as a dynamic, strategic capability rather than a static tool.

A truly quantum-resilient future depends on four pillars:

- **Executive commitment:** Boards and C-suites must recognize quantum risk as a critical business issue and champion proactive investment in readiness initiatives [3].

- **Cross-functional collaboration:** IT, cybersecurity, legal, compliance, and business units must align to implement crypto-inventory management, agile governance, and seamless transitions [4].

- **Standards and innovation adoption:** Organizations must embrace NIST's post-quantum cryptographic standards and explore advanced tools like crypto-agility and quantum-safe key management to ensure resilience [5].

- **Continuous improvement:** Readiness isn't a one-off effort. It requires ongoing monitoring, upskilling, and iterative improvements, guided by crypto-agility from the start.

Looking ahead, those who act early will gain protection as well as strategic advantage. Just as early adopters of cloud and artificial intelligence (AI) shaped the future of digital business, today's quantum-safe pioneers will lead the next era of secure, intelligent enterprise.

The quantum era is near. The time to act—both to defend and to lead—is now [6].

Quantum Safe at the Intersection of Emerging Technologies

As enterprises accelerate their digital transformation journeys, emerging technologies are becoming both enablers of innovation and sources of disruption. Organizations increasingly seek to harness these technologies to drive operational efficiency, differentiate themselves in the marketplace, and deliver enhanced customer value. This pursuit is powered by a dynamic ecosystem of technology providers offering cutting-edge capabilities.

Technologies such as AI, cloud computing, edge computing, 5G, the IoT, and blockchain are no longer experimental; they are integral to how businesses operate, compete, and evolve. At the heart of these digital systems lies cryptography, ensuring the confidentiality, integrity, identity, and trust that underpin secure digital interactions.

However, the advent of quantum computing poses a significant and growing threat to this foundation. Quantum algorithms are expected to break many of the cryptographic protocols that secure today's digital ecosystems. Without proactive adaptation, enterprises risk exposing their most critical data, processes, and assets to systemic vulnerabilities.

This section explores how quantum-safe principles must be embedded across 10 strategic emerging technology domains (see Figure 9-1). Doing so is essential to ensuring resilient, future-ready innovation in a quantum-enabled world [7].

Artificial Intelligence: Deep Learning, Machine Learning, Generative AI, and Agentic AI

AI is reshaping the enterprise landscape, accelerating innovation, and redefining competitive advantage. From predictive analytics and real-time personalization to autonomous operations and intelligent decision-making,

AI is now a critical driver of transformation across industries. Machine learning models are trained on vast, often sensitive datasets and are continuously refined with dynamic inputs. Deep learning fuels advances in natural language processing, speech recognition, and computer vision, and generative and agentic AI extend these capabilities by creating human-like content and enabling autonomous, multisystem interactions.

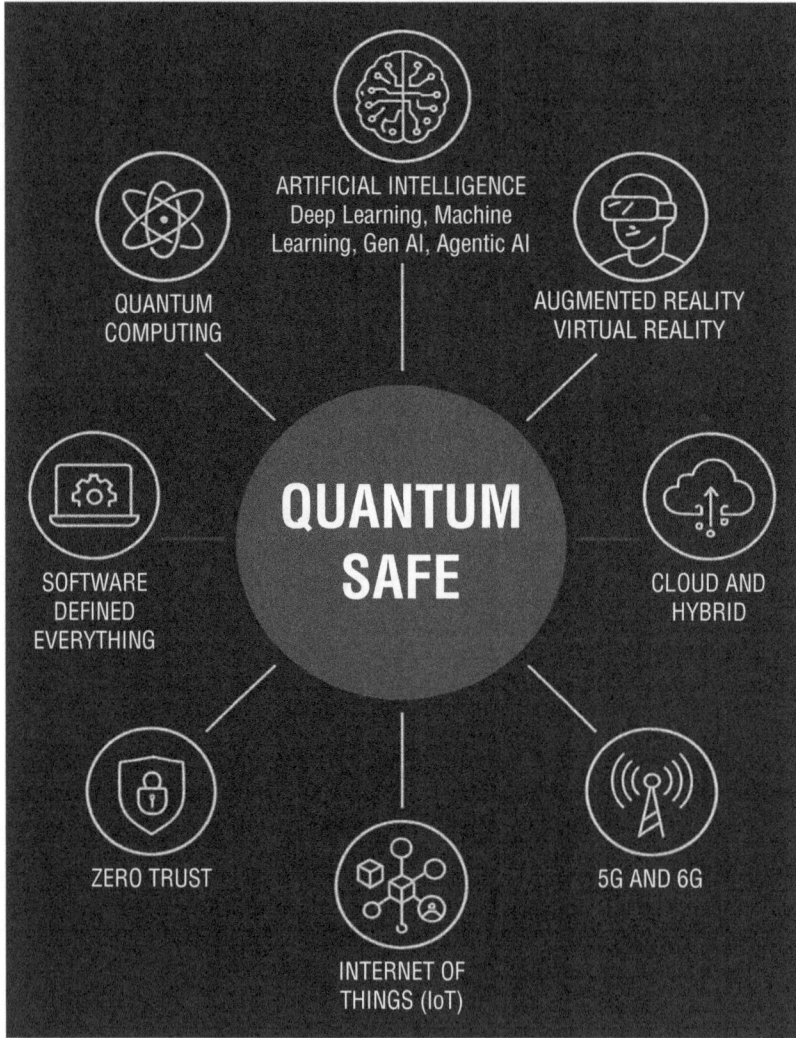

Figure 9-1: Intersection of quantum safe and emerging technologies

These AI systems are only as trustworthy as the infrastructure supporting them. Today's AI relies on secure data pipelines, cryptographic signing of models, authenticated APIs, and encryption mechanisms to protect inputs, outputs, and model integrity. But this trust is fragile in the face of quantum computing.

A post-quantum threat environment dramatically changes the calculus. Quantum-capable adversaries could decrypt confidential training data, forge digital signatures on AI models, manipulate inference results, or inject adversarial code during training. The consequences are severe, ranging from regulatory violations and loss of competitive IP to model poisoning and real-world harm in mission-critical domains like healthcare, finance, defense, and autonomous mobility.

To mitigate these risks, organizations must act now to integrate quantum-safe cryptography across the entire AI lifecycle:

- **Post-quantum Transport Layer Security (TLS)** secures data in transit during training, inference, and API access.

- **Quantum-resistant digital signatures** validate the integrity and provenance of models, updates, and agent actions.

- **Crypto-agile AI architectures** enable seamless migration as cryptographic standards evolve, reducing technical debt and disruption.

- **Secure model pipelines** ensure confidentiality, availability, and trust in federated learning, edge AI, and multiagent deployments.

The regulatory landscape is also evolving. Upcoming mandates on AI transparency, data protection, and algorithmic accountability will increasingly intersect with cryptographic resilience, making quantum-safe readiness a matter of both security and compliance [8].

To maintain trust, performance, and innovation at scale, enterprises must embed quantum-safe principles into every phase of AI development, deployment, and governance. In the quantum era, securing AI is not just a technical imperative—it's a strategic one. The future of intelligent systems will be shaped by those who secure their foundations today.

Augmented Reality (AR) and Virtual Reality (VR)

AR and VR technologies are rapidly advancing from experimental tools to mainstream enterprise platforms. They now enable immersive training, design visualization, remote collaboration, and real-time digital twin simulations, bridging the physical and digital worlds to enhance engagement, accuracy, and productivity. Across sectors such as defense, manufacturing, healthcare, retail, and logistics, AR/VR is unlocking new efficiencies and transforming how people interact with complex systems.

These platforms operate through continuous data capture, real-time rendering, and low-latency transmission, processing vast amounts of sensitive information such as spatial maps, biometric identifiers, proprietary blueprints, and user behavioral data. To protect these immersive environments, current systems rely on encrypted communications, secure device authentication, and digital content licensing.

However, in a post-quantum threat landscape, the cryptographic foundations supporting these protections are at risk. Quantum-capable adversaries could decrypt real-time AR/VR sessions, steal confidential designs, manipulate immersive content, or inject adversarial assets, leading to safety concerns, reputational damage, and potential sabotage in mission-critical simulations.

Quantum-safe readiness is essential to preserving trust, safety, and value in immersive enterprise deployments. This includes the following:

- Embedding lightweight post-quantum algorithms into AR/VR SDKs to secure latency-sensitive communications without performance degradation

- Using quantum-resistant digital rights management (DRM) to protect proprietary content from piracy, tampering, or unauthorized redistribution

- Signing firmware and software updates for headsets, sensors, and AR/VR platforms with post-quantum certificates to prevent malicious code injection

- Enforcing quantum-safe identity authentication within virtual environments to ensure that users, avatars, and digital content can be reliably verified

As AR/VR technologies become deeply integrated into enterprise workflows and customer experiences, ensuring their integrity in the quantum era is not optional—it's foundational. Forward-looking organizations must integrate quantum-safe principles today to build immersive, trusted, and future-proof digital environments [9].

Cloud and Hybrid Environments

Cloud and hybrid cloud environments are the digital backbone of modern enterprises, supporting everything from mission-critical applications and analytics platforms to development pipelines and customer-facing services. Deployed across public, private, and multicloud infrastructures, these environments enable agility, scalability, and innovation—but also introduce new layers of complexity and security risk.

At the core of cloud security lies cryptography. TLS secures communication between distributed services; key management systems protect data encryption keys; identity federation and access control mechanisms rely on certificates, tokens, and digital signatures to enforce trust and segmentation. These cryptographic controls are fundamental to data privacy, service integrity, and regulatory compliance.

If this cryptographic foundation is threatened, the consequences include large-scale data breaches, unauthorized access to cloud resources, cross-tenant data exposure, and disruption of core cloud services, along with potential regulatory violations under frameworks like GDPR, HIPAA, and PCI-DSS.

Quantum-safe readiness in cloud environments requires a strategic, end-to-end transformation of the cryptographic stack, including the following:

- **Implementation of post-quantum TLS protocols** across cloud load balancers, ingress controllers, APIs, and microservices to secure service-to-service communication

- **Adoption of hybrid cryptographic techniques** that combine classical and quantum-resistant algorithms to ensure compatibility during the transition phase

- **Modernization of key management systems** to support crypto-agile operations, allowing dynamic algorithm replacement, seamless key rotations, and multitenant policy enforcement at scale

- **Quantum-resilient identity and access frameworks** that secure federated authentication, token issuance, and authorization mechanisms with post-quantum signatures and encryption

- **Collaborative engagement with cloud service providers** to integrate post-quantum safeguards across shared responsibility boundaries, ensuring consistent protection across cloud-native stacks, legacy workloads, and edge deployments [10]

As quantum threats become increasingly real, cloud security strategies must evolve beyond perimeter controls and legacy encryption. Organizations that proactively embed quantum-safe principles into their cloud architectures will protect their digital infrastructure and also gain long-term resilience, compliance assurance, and a competitive edge in secure innovation.

Intelligent Edge Computing

Edge computing is revolutionizing how data is processed, analyzed, and acted on, bringing computation closer to users, sensors, and devices to reduce latency, optimize bandwidth, and enable real-time decision-making. Whether in connected vehicles, industrial IoT networks, healthcare monitors, or smart city infrastructure, edge nodes are powering mission-critical operations that cannot depend on continuous cloud connectivity.

However, edge environments are uniquely vulnerable. Devices often operate in semi-trusted or physically exposed locations, with limited compute power, memory, and energy resources. To maintain trust, these systems depend on cryptographic protections such as digital certificates for identity, encrypted telemetry for data integrity, and signed firmware for software authenticity.

In a post-quantum threat landscape, these foundational protections are at risk. Quantum-capable adversaries could exploit weakened encryption and signing algorithms to impersonate legitimate devices, inject malicious commands, or disrupt autonomous control systems. Attack scenarios include intercepting telemetry from energy grids, tampering with equipment behavior on factory floors, or compromising navigation logic in autonomous vehicles, leading to safety incidents, downtime, and reputational damage.

Quantum-safe edge computing requires a fundamental upgrade to its cryptographic foundations, with an emphasis on security, efficiency, and scalability:

- **Deploy lightweight post-quantum cryptographic libraries** designed for resource-constrained processors, enabling secure operations without impacting device performance.

- **Use post-quantum digital signatures** (such as lattice- or hash-based schemes) to verify firmware and software updates, preventing code injection or rollback attacks.

- **Enhance mutual authentication protocols** at the edge using quantum-resistant algorithms to validate identity and secure communications between devices and control systems.

- **Leverage hardware-based security features**—such as secure enclaves, trusted platform modules (TPM), or dedicated key storage modules—to protect private keys from physical and software-based extraction.

- **Establish scalable crypto-agile update frameworks** that enable policy-driven, phased deployment of quantum-safe updates across millions of distributed endpoints, including those operating intermittently or in low-bandwidth environments.

As edge computing becomes central to real-time operations and autonomous decision-making, its cryptographic integrity will define the reliability and safety of critical systems. Future-ready organizations must proactively architect edge deployments with quantum safety in mind, ensuring continuity, resilience, and trust across the expanding edge ecosystem.

5G and 6G Networks

The rollout of 5G—and the anticipated emergence of 6G—marks a fundamental transformation in global connectivity. These next-generation wireless networks support ultra-low latency, massive device density, and high-throughput data transfer, enabling advanced use cases such as autonomous transportation, smart manufacturing, remote surgery, and immersive extended reality (XR). As telecommunications infrastructure becomes increasingly central to national security, economic competitiveness, and digital society, ensuring its resilience is a top priority.

Telecom networks rely on a layered cryptographic architecture to secure communications, authenticate devices, and manage access. Subscriber identity modules (SIMs), base stations, and virtualized network functions use digital certificates and encryption keys to establish trust, protect signaling protocols, and secure over-the-air provisioning. With the adoption of software-defined networking (SDN) and network slicing in 5G and beyond, cryptography is also essential to isolating services, tenants, and data flows.

However, quantum computing threatens to undermine these protections. Once mature, quantum algorithms could break widely used asymmetric cryptographic schemes, enabling attackers to eavesdrop on communications, forge device identities, spoof network components, or disrupt critical services at both the core and the edge of the network.

A quantum-safe approach to telecommunications security must include proactive upgrades across devices, infrastructure, and standards, including the following:

- **Post-quantum authentication protocols** for SIM cards, user equipment, base stations, and control plane signaling to prevent spoofing and impersonation

- **Post-quantum cryptography (PQC)- and hybrid-enabled VPN and IPsec protocols** in core, backhaul, and edge transport layers to secure data in transit across heterogeneous network paths

- **Crypto-agile firmware and software architectures** in network equipment and orchestration layers to support seamless algorithm updates as new standards evolve

- **Quantum-safe TLS and secure APIs** in mobile edge computing platforms to protect applications deployed close to the user, such as real-time analytics, AI inference, and XR rendering

- **Integration of post-quantum readiness into international telecom standards bodies** (e.g., 3rd Generation Partnership Projects [3GPP], ETSI [11], International Telecommunication Union [ITU] [12]) to ensure long-term trust and interoperability across global 5G and 6G deployments

- **Cross-sector and public-private collaboration** to align regulatory mandates, risk models, and investment in quantum-resilient telecom infrastructure [13]

As wireless networks evolve into intelligent, adaptive platforms underpinning critical national infrastructure, their cryptographic backbone must evolve in parallel. Post-quantum readiness is no longer a theoretical concern—it is a foundational requirement for the next era of secure, hyperconnected communications.

Internet of Things (IoT)

The IoT ecosystem now comprises tens of billions of interconnected devices, from consumer wearables and smart home appliances to industrial sensors and mission-critical infrastructure. These endpoints generate high-value telemetry, drive automation, and power predictive maintenance capabilities across diverse sectors. However, their proliferation introduces a significant and often overlooked risk: they constitute one of the most cryptographically fragile layers within enterprise and critical infrastructure environments.

Most IoT devices operate under stringent resource constraints, leading manufacturers to adopt lightweight or even hardcoded cryptographic implementations. Many lack support for secure firmware updates, making post-deployment remediation difficult or impossible. Common vulnerabilities include insecure key provisioning, poor entropy sources, weak random number generation, and reliance on deprecated cryptographic protocols. These issues create a broad and attractive attack surface. In the post-quantum era, a sufficiently capable adversary could exploit these weaknesses to exfiltrate credentials, manipulate device behavior, or launch large-scale service disruptions.

Quantum-resilient IoT strategies must begin with a foundation of security-by-design. This includes cryptographically verifiable firmware, secure boot processes, and tamper-resistant hardware elements capable of performing post-quantum key generation and digital signing. Security must extend throughout the device lifecycle, encompassing secure provisioning, authenticated onboarding, key rotation, and robust over-the-air (OTA) update mechanisms fortified with post-quantum protections [14].

At the infrastructure level, IoT device management platforms must implement quantum-safe mutual authentication, encrypted telemetry channels, integrity validation, and dynamic policy enforcement. Scalable support for PQC is essential for future-proofing device fleets and mitigating the long-term risk of "harvest now and decrypt later" (HNDL) attacks.

As IoT becomes an operational backbone across industries, cryptographic agility is no longer optional: it is a core requirement. Enterprises must prioritize vendors and architectures that offer seamless migration paths to quantum-safe primitives, enabling proactive resilience in the face of rapidly evolving threat landscapes.

Zero Trust

Zero trust architecture redefines enterprise security by eliminating implicit trust and enforcing continuous verification of user identity, device posture, and contextual signals. Its core principles include strict access controls, end-to-end encryption, and policy-driven enforcement mechanisms. Designed to support cloud-native applications, remote workforces, and microsegmentation, zero trust ensures that access is granted based on dynamic risk rather than static perimeter defenses.

However, zero trust frameworks fundamentally rely on public-key cryptography to secure authentication, authorization, and data exchange. Certificates, tokens, and encrypted tunnels serve as the foundation for establishing and enforcing trust boundaries. In a post-quantum scenario, the cryptographic algorithms underpinning these elements could be broken, allowing adversaries to decrypt traffic, forge credentials, hijack sessions, or impersonate trusted entities.

To ensure the long-term resilience of zero trust models, quantum-safe cryptography must be integrated into their foundations. Post-quantum public-key infrastructures (PQ-PKIs) must replace traditional certificate authorities, enabling the issuance of credentials that resist quantum attacks. Identity providers and access management systems must adopt hybrid or fully post-quantum algorithms to validate users, devices, and services. Likewise, VPNs and microsegmentation platforms must evolve to support PQC-enabled tunnels and access gateways [15].

By embedding cryptographic agility into the core of zero trust, enterprises can preserve the integrity, scalability, and policy enforcement of the model, even as quantum threats materialize.

Blockchain and Decentralized Identity

Blockchain platforms underpin decentralized applications in finance, supply chain, and identity management. These systems rely on cryptographic signatures to validate transactions, enforce consensus, and secure smart contracts. Decentralized identity solutions use public keys to issue and verify credentials without central authorities.

Classical signature schemes such as the elliptic curve digital signature algorithm (ECDSA) and Rivest-Shamir-Adleman (RSA) are at risk in the quantum era. If broken, attackers could forge transactions, reverse consensus, and impersonate digital identities. The immutability of blockchain could be compromised, and user trust in decentralized ecosystems could collapse.

Transitioning blockchain systems to post-quantum signature algorithms is a complex but necessary evolution. Hash-based, lattice-based, and multivariate schemes offer potential alternatives, each with trade-offs in key size, verification speed, and interoperability. Blockchain protocols must support hybrid transactions during migration [16]. Decentralized identity frameworks must adopt post-quantum key issuance and revocation mechanisms [17]. Enterprises building on blockchain must engage with standards bodies and developer communities to prioritize quantum-safe upgrades, ensuring continued trust and compliance in decentralized ecosystems [18].

Software-Defined Everything

Software-defined infrastructure (SDx) abstracts core IT functions—including networking, storage, compute, and security—into programmable, policy-driven interfaces. By decoupling hardware from control logic, SDx enables enterprises to increase agility, reduce operational costs, and automate at scale across hybrid and multicloud environments. Centralized controllers enforce dynamic policies through encrypted communications, cryptographically signed configurations, and secure APIs.

These programmable systems depend on strong cryptographic protections to safeguard control plane interactions, orchestration workflows, and service-to-service communications. Compromise of these cryptographic primitives—especially under a quantum-capable adversary—could result in catastrophic outcomes: unauthorized infrastructure reconfiguration, malicious workload injection, denial-of-service, or persistent control plane subversion.

To future-proof SDx environments, enterprises must embed quantum-safe cryptography into the foundational layers of orchestration and infrastructure management. This includes upgrading platforms like Kubernetes, Terraform, and SDN controllers with post-quantum secure APIs, authentication mechanisms, and control messages. API gateways must support PQC-based mutual authentication and integrate with service meshes that encrypt internal communications using quantum-resistant protocols.

Infrastructure-as-code (IaC) pipelines must evolve to sign artifacts, manifests, and deployment templates using PQC schemes. DevSecOps workflows should integrate crypto-agile tooling into CI/CD pipelines, enabling continuous validation, compliance, and seamless cryptographic migration.

As enterprises advance toward autonomous infrastructure and AI-driven operations, the integrity and confidentiality of software-defined interfaces become mission critical. Ensuring that these systems are quantum-resilient is not merely a best practice: it is a prerequisite for securing the programmable backbone of digital transformation.

Quantum Computing

Ironically, and critically, quantum computing itself must be secured with quantum-safe cryptography. Enterprises exploring quantum technologies for advanced simulation, optimization, and machine learning increasingly rely on hybrid architectures, cloud-based quantum access, and proprietary quantum algorithms. As these capabilities mature, they introduce new security challenges that classical cryptographic tools will soon be ill-equipped to handle.

Quantum computing platforms expose sensitive interfaces—APIs for job submission, identity verification, and resource orchestration—all of which require robust protection against unauthorized access and manipulation. Furthermore, the intellectual property encoded in quantum circuits, algorithms, and compiled workloads must be shielded from theft, tampering, or reverse engineering. Classical cryptographic schemes, although foundational today, are not future-proof in the face of quantum adversaries.

Ensuring quantum-safe readiness in this domain involves embedding PQC protections across the quantum-classical ecosystem. Hybrid workflows must utilize PQC-based encryption and digital signatures to secure data in transit and data at rest. Identity and access management (IAM) systems must adopt quantum-resistant credentials to authenticate users, devices, and workloads. Quantum-as-a-Service (QaaS) providers must deliver end-to-end assurances of cryptographic integrity, from client interaction to quantum hardware execution [19].

For enterprises, proactively investing in quantum-safe security for quantum computing is not just prudent: it's essential to protect competitive advantage and long-term innovation. Safeguarding quantum platforms ensures that the transformative benefits of quantum technologies are realized without introducing new cryptographic liabilities.

By embedding quantum-safe principles across emerging technologies—including quantum computing—organizations can harden their digital foundations, protect intellectual capital, and lead with resilience into the quantum era.

Quantum Computing Roadmap

Securing quantum computing is one side of the coin, but the other side is the progress being made in the field of quantum computing by technology leaders. The global race toward fault-tolerant quantum computing is intensifying, with these leaders mapping out timelines that extend across hardware innovation, error correction breakthroughs, and full-stack integration [20]. All these are essential for the realization of a cryptographically relevant quantum computer (CRQC) that is capable of breaking encryption:

- **IBM Quantum: road to "Starling" by 2029:** In May 2025, the company unveiled a comprehensive roadmap targeting deployment of IBM Quantum Starling: a modular, fault-tolerant system capable of handling 200 logical qubits and executing 100 million quantum gates by 2029. Hosted in Poughkeepsie, NY, this ambitious platform will be preceded by development milestones: 2025's Loon chip, 2026's Kookaburra, and 2027's Cockatoo, all emphasizing real-time decoding, modular low-density parity check (LDPC) error-correction, and scalable architectures. IBM called out that it has "de-risked" the engineering challenges and that its clear, iterative development process gives it confidence for meeting the 2029 target [21].

- **Quantinuum: universal, fault-tolerant by 2030:** Quantinuum, which uses trapped-ion technology, released its "Apollo" roadmap in 2024, aiming for universal, fault-tolerant capabilities by 2030 with hundreds of logical qubits. Having already demonstrated 12 logical qubits earlier in partnership with Microsoft, the company emphasizes high fidelity and ion-trap modularity as its core strategy [22].

- **Google Willow chip and road to scale:** Google's Willow processor (105 qubits) claims to have achieved below-threshold error correction in late 2024, an important noisy intermediate-scale quantum-era (NISQ) milestone. This doesn't constitute fault-tolerance, but it's a major step forward in scaling error suppression, although full universality remains a future goal [23].

- **Microsoft Majorana 1 and topological vision:** Microsoft is pursuing a unique topological qubit strategy via its Majorana 1 prototype, using qubit-native error resistance. This foundational work sets the stage for inherently more fault-tolerant quantum architectures, although commercial timelines remain broadly sketched.

The "so what?" of these roadmaps and what they point toward is the following:

- IBM's roadmap is the most detailed and imminent; early fault-tolerant access (~2029) could enable commercial use in optimization, materials science, and cryptography.

- Various approaches are being adopted: trapped-ion (Quantinuum), LDPC/surface-code superconductors (IBM, Google), topological qubits (Microsoft), each with unique integration ecosystems.

- Enterprises should monitor these timelines closely. First movers in quantum-safe cryptography and quantum-powered services are likely to gain a significant competitive edge.

This chapter brings the journey of this book full circle, revealing the tangible intersections between PQC and today's most transformative digital innovations. From AI and AR/VR to cloud computing, edge infrastructure, and the IoT, cryptography is the invisible backbone of every digital interaction. In a world increasingly vulnerable to quantum threats, these foundations must be rebuilt using quantum-safe tools: stronger, more adaptable, and resilient by design. This transformation is neither optional nor far off; it is an immediate imperative with far-reaching implications.

The way forward begins with crypto-agility: the organizational ability to swiftly adapt to new cryptographic standards and maintain operational resilience amid disruption. Achieving quantum-safe readiness demands executive commitment, comprehensive system upgrades, proactive vendor collaboration, and cross-functional alignment between security, IT, and business leaders.

As we conclude, the call to action is clear: treat cryptographic modernization as a strategic advantage, not a technical afterthought. Early adopters will secure their operations while also earning trust, ensuring compliance, and positioning themselves for long-term leadership [24].

Use this chapter—and the book as a whole—as a pragmatic guide for navigating this transformation. Start now. Lead with vision. Prioritize cryptographic agility. Guide your enterprise into the quantum-powered future where security is not just preserved but reimagined.

Key Takeaways for Business and Technology Leaders

The following takeaways distill the most critical insights to help you future-proof your organization in the face of quantum disruption:

- **The quantum threat is real—and closer than you think.**
  Quantum computing will render today's cryptographic protections obsolete. This is not a distant concern; the risk is accelerating. Business and technology leaders must act now to avoid strategic, regulatory, and reputational fallout [25].

- **Crypto-agility is the foundation of future security.**
  In an era of rapid cryptographic change, adaptability is non-negotiable. Crypto-agility—the ability to swiftly switch cryptographic algorithms—must be embedded into your infrastructure, CI/CD pipelines, authentication frameworks, and vendor ecosystems.

- **All digital innovation depends on secure cryptography.**
  AI, IoT, cloud, blockchain, edge computing—every emerging technology relies on cryptographic trust. As quantum capabilities advance, these interconnected systems require new, quantum-resistant safeguards to preserve integrity and confidentiality.

- **Leadership alignment and cross-functional collaboration are essential.**
  Quantum-safe transformation is a business imperative, not just a technical one. Success hinges on executive sponsorship, empowered CISOs, board-level visibility, and integrated action across security, IT, risk, legal, and operations [26].

- **This book is your strategic playbook.**
  Chapters 1 through 9 provide a practical framework for quantum-safe readiness, from foundational concepts to enterprise-wide execution. Use this book to benchmark your current posture, chart your roadmap, and build resilience into your organizational DNA.

Your Journey to Becoming Quantum Safe

This book was written not simply as a reference but as a strategic call to action. In an era defined by disruption, quantum computing represents one of the most profound shifts in the digital landscape. Its implications for cybersecurity are vast and imminent. Forward-looking executives who grasp the urgency and commit to crypto-agility will be the ones who navigate this transition with confidence and resilience. Whether you're modernizing cloud workloads, scaling AI solutions, expanding edge and IoT ecosystems, or strengthening zero trust frameworks, integrating quantum-safe principles is no longer optional—it's a critical operational necessity.

Quantum risk is not a distant technical challenge; it is a business risk with regulatory, reputational, and operational consequences. Treat it as you would any other strategic threat: with executive attention, enterprise-wide coordination, and a bias for action. Crypto-agility is your insurance policy in a volatile cryptographic landscape: an enabler of adaptability, continuity, and trust. PQC is more than a defensive upgrade; it is the new foundation on which digital trust, privacy, and compliance will be built [27].

This book has equipped you with the frameworks, insights, and practical guidance needed to assess your current state, mobilize key stakeholders, and build a roadmap to quantum safety. The future will reward those who act early—those who see cryptographic modernization not as a burden but as a differentiator. Now the baton is in your hands.

Lead with clarity. Empower your teams. Invest in resilience. The quantum future is accelerating toward us. Let this be your moment to rise to the challenge and shape a future that is secure, agile, and built to last.

We wish you a successful journey toward quantum safety and crypto-agility.

References

(1) What Happens When 'If' Turns to 'When' in Quantum Computing?, https://web-assets.bcg.com/89/00/d2d074424 a6ca820b1238e24ccc0/bcg-what-happens-when-if-turns-to- when-in-quantum-computing-jul-2021-r.pdf.

(2) NIST SP 1800-38, Migration to Post-Quantum Cryptography: Preparation for Considering the Implementation and Adoption of Quantum Safe Cryptography (Draft), https://csrc.nist .gov/pubs/sp/1800/38/iprd-(1).

(3) MITRE, Quantum-Safe Readiness Framework, https://www.linkedin.com/pulse/mitres-roadmap-post-quantum-cryptography-derrick-sturisky-flcce.

(4) NIST Cybersecurity Framework (CSF) 2.0, https://www.nist.gov/cyberframework.

(5) NIST Post-Quantum Cryptography Project, https://csrc.nist.gov/projects/post-quantum-cryptography.

(6) World Economic Forum, Quantum Security Whitepapers, https://initiatives.weforum.org/quantum/security.

(7) ENISA, Post-Quantum Cryptography: Current state and quantum mitigation, https://www.enisa.europa.eu/publications/post-quantum-cryptography-current-state-and-quantum-mitigation.

(8) OECD AI Policy Observatory, AI security and risk framework, https://oecd.ai/en.

(9) XR Association, Privacy and security framework for AR/VR, https://xra.org.

(10) Cloud Security Alliance (CSA), Quantum-Safe Security working group, https://cloudsecurityalliance.org/research/working-groups/quantum-safe-security.

(11) ETSI GS QSC, Quantum Safe Cryptography standard, https://www.etsi.org/technologies/quantum-safe-cryptography.

(12) ITU, Standardization in Quantum Information Technology, https://www.itu.int/en/ITU-T/focusgroups/qit4n.

(13) GSMA, Quantum Computing & Telco Readiness Whitepaper, https://www.gsma.com/solutions-and-impact/technologies/security/post-quantum.

(14) NIST SP 800-213, IoT Device Cybersecurity Guidance for the Federal Government: Establishing IoT Device Cybersecurity Requirements, https://csrc.nist.gov/publications/detail/sp/800-213/final.

(15) IETF PQC Mailing List, Standards Development for PQC Internet Protocols, https://www.ietf.org/archive/id/draft-reddy-uta-pqc-app-03.html.

(16) Hyperledger Foundation, PQC Migration for Blockchain Networks, `https://www.researchgate.net/publication/392025711_` `Enhancing_Hyperledger_Fabric_Security_with_Lightweight_` `Post-Quantum_Cryptography_and_National_Cryptographic_` `Algorithms.`

(17) Ethereum Research, Post-quantum cryptography proposals, `https://ethresear.ch.`

(18) NISTIR 8301, Blockchain Networks and Post-Quantum Cryptography, `https://csrc.nist.gov/publications/detail/` `nistir/8301/final.`

(19) Azure Quantum Computing, Microsoft Azure, `https://azure` `.microsoft.com/en-us/solutions/` `quantum-computing/#Overview.`

(20) McKinsey & Company, The Quantum Advantage Playbook, `https://www.mckinsey.com/capabilities/` `mckinsey-digital/our-insights/` `steady-progress-in-approaching-the-quantum-advantage.`

(21) IBM, Expanding the IBM Quantum roadmap to anticipate the future of quantum-centric supercomputing, `https://research` `.ibm.com/blog/ibm-quantum-roadmap-2025.`

(22) Quantinuum, Newsroom, `https://www.quantinuum.com/news.`

(23) Google Quantum AI, `https://quantumai.google.`

(24) IDC, Quantum computing market analysis and risk reports (access via subscription), `https://www.idc.com.`

(25) Gartner, Quantum computing, AI security, and cryptography reports (access via subscription), `https://www.gartner.com.`

(26) House Oversight Committee, Preparing for the Quantum Age: When Cryptography Breaks (US Congressional Hearing), `https://oversight.house.gov/hearing/` `preparing-for-the-quantum-age-when-cryptography-` `breaks.`

(27) Forrester, Securing the future against quantum threats (access via subscription), `https://www.forrester.com.`

Acknowledgments

The journey to *Becoming Quantum Safe* has been nothing short of extraordinary. The quantum-safe space, in just the past few years, has been one of the most exciting, challenging, and encouraging frontiers in technology. It has been a field where science meets urgency, innovation meets practicality, and vision meets the hard work of execution. The three of us—Jai, Ray, and Walid—have not only deepened our knowledge but also been fortunate to receive unwavering support from remarkable leaders, colleagues, and collaborators who have made this mission both possible and deeply fulfilling.

We begin with heartfelt thanks to the leadership of IBM, whose vision and commitment to technology's next frontiers have been a constant source of inspiration. **Arvind Krishna, Dario Gil, Alessandro Curioni, Sriram Raghavan, Ramesh Gopinath, Rob Thomas, Dinesh Nirmal, Kareem Yusuf, Roger Premo, Mohamad Ali, Sandip Patel, Mark Hughes, Jamie Thomas, Suja Viswesan**, and **Vishal Kamat**—each of you, in your own way, has propelled the Quantum Safe mission forward. Your confidence in us and in this cause has not only shaped the work we've done but also reinforced our belief that the security of the future must be built today.

A special note of gratitude goes to **Scott Crowder** and **Jay Gambetta**, whose leadership in quantum computing has been pivotal. You didn't just give us the mandate to create a quantum-safe market—you gave us the freedom to experiment, the encouragement to take risks, and the guidance to make the right decisions at the right moments. You made the work a pleasure, even when the problems were complex and the stakes were high.

179

We also owe deep thanks to **J.R. Rao** and **Sridhar Muppidi**, both IBM Fellows, both luminaries in cybersecurity, and both wise mentors who have been, to us, like elders in a close-knit family. Your counsel has been both pragmatic and visionary, helping us navigate not just the technology but also the broader mission. Similarly, **Koos Lodewijkx**, IBM's CISO, has enriched our thinking through candid, insightful discussions that consistently yielded new perspectives—many of which have found their way into the pages of this book.

Our appreciation extends to the many IBM colleagues whose expertise, collaboration, and dedication to advancing cryptographic research have inspired us. From the Zurich Research Lab: **Marc Stoecklin, Michael Osborne, Vadim Lyubashevsky, Gregor Seilor, Ward Beullens, Chris Giblin, Silvio Dragone, Gero Dittmann, Basil Hess, Navaneeth Rameshan, Martin Schmatz**, and **Nicklas Kortge**. From the Haifa Research Lab: **Eyal Bin, Anatoly Koyfman, Micha Moffie, Omer Boehm**, and **Oleg Blinder**. Your pioneering work has helped push the boundaries of what's possible in this field.

Our gratitude also goes to **Gregg Barrow** and **Antti Ropponen** from IBM Consulting; **Charles Robinson** and **James Keegan** from Research Business Development, **Ian Wight** and **Albert Puah** from IBM Technology Sales, whose client engagement insights helped us bridge the gap between cutting-edge research and real-world adoption. Deep appreciation for other leaders' support of the Quantum Safe mission, including **Anne Dames** and **Kyle Brown** from IBM and **Cherylin Pasco, Lily Chen**, and **Bill Newhouse** from NCCoE, NIST.

The IBM Quantum Safe Incubation Team—**Joachim Schaefer**, Srinivasa **Raghavan G, James McGugan, Chenna Govindasamy, Lory Thorpe, Zygmunt Lozinski, Ajay Kulkarni, Tanay Guha, Shilpa Shetty, Radhika Lakshmegowda, Soumya Dalvi, Christine Vu**—and the Guardium Team—**Amy Wong, Tim Richer, Yogendra Soni, Puneet Sharma, Prashant Mestry, Barbara Saltzman, Kuber Saraswat, Kiran Subba Rao, Chaitanya Challa, Sridhar Narayanan, Ravi Simha Reddy, Vinaya Patil, Hannah Chong, Ivana Pham**—deserve special recognition. You came together in the spirit of collaboration, curiosity, and mutual support, learning from each other and quickly becoming experts in an area that was evolving almost daily. Working alongside such a committed group has been both an honor and a privilege.

A sincere thank-you to **John Buselli** for the countless thought-provoking conversations about everything quantum safe—especially your perspectives on the importance of ecosystems and consortia. Your ability to think beyond the immediate horizon enriched our own vision for the future of this technology.

Ray Shieh—your creative marketing and demand generation leadership have been instrumental in helping clients and partners understand, appreciate, and adopt quantum-safe technologies. You have helped translate a highly technical vision into a compelling story that resonates with diverse audiences.

Jennifer Janechek—your editorial skill, attention to detail, and willingness to challenge us to be sharper, clearer, and more impactful took this work to the next level. We deeply appreciate not only your expertise but also your humanity and generosity throughout this process.

Ray would like to thank all his **mentees** . . . over the years there have been many. He learned many things from them and their experiences. They informed his approach and outlook to handle whatever came his way. Ray would also like to remember and acknowledge with appreciation all the **mentors** he has had in his professional career. While every one of them has guided and molded him, the one to call out with deep gratitude is **John Kelly**, Executive Vice President (Retired), IBM, who has been a sounding board and a steady guide to Ray throughout his 25+ years at IBM.

Walid would like to extend personal thanks to **Mick Gray**, GSKit Architect, IBM; **Greg Stager**, DB2 Security Architect, IBM; **John Peck**, Java Security Architect, IBM; **Andriy Miranskyy**, Professor, Toronto Metropolitan University; and **Lei Zhang**, Professor, University of Maryland Baltimore County, for your outstanding contributions to the DB2 Quantum Safe project. Your technical depth, collaborative spirit, and innovative ideas were vital to bringing this work to life.

Jai would like to take a moment for a more personal reflection. The foundations for his career were laid in the classrooms of **Sanskrit School** and **Multipurpose Senior Secondary School** in Bharatpur, where teachers instilled a love for mathematics and science. That foundation was strengthened by his professors at **MANIT Bhopal** and **VJTI Mumbai**, who deepened his knowledge of computer science and engineering. At the **Tata Institute of Fundamental Research (TIFR)**, he was inspired by **Padma Shri Dr. P.V.S. Rao** and **A. Sen** during the early days of artificial intelligence research and guided by **Dr. R.K. Shyamasundar** (now Professor at IIT Mumbai) in networking and cybersecurity—learning not just theory, but the practical realities of enterprise security operations.

Jai also wishes to thank his colleagues from across 25 years in industry—at TIFR, IBM, Unisys, and the startup Diablo Technologies.

Each team, each project, and each challenge added layers to his understanding of cybersecurity, cryptography, and the importance of resilience. And to the industry clients and partners—thank you for the opportunities to learn from your challenges and your visions, often pushing the boundaries of what was thought possible. He also acknowledges the continued inspiration and guidance of his mentors, including **Ashesh Badani, Barry Baker, Sanjay Tripathi, Jason Slibergleit,** and **Tarun Chopra**.

We extend our sincere gratitude to the Wiley team—Jim Minatel, Satish Gowrishankar, Saravanan Dakshinamurthy, Annie Melnick, Tiffany Taylor, and Kim Wimpsett for their expertise, dedication, and unwavering support. Their professionalism, attention to detail, and collaborative spirit were instrumental in refining, shaping, and bringing this book to publication with clarity, precision, and excellence.

Finally, this book, and indeed the entire mission of becoming quantum safe, is as much about people as it is about technology. It is about a shared belief that our digital future must be secure, trustworthy, and resilient. It is about the scientists who invent, the engineers who build, the business leaders who champion adoption, the educators who train the next generation, and the clients who trust us to safeguard what matters most to them.

To all who have walked this path with us—whether your contribution is named here or known only in our hearts—we offer our deepest thanks. Your insights, your encouragement, your constructive challenges, and your faith in this mission have been the constant wind at our backs.

The work of becoming quantum safe is not finished; it is, in fact, just beginning. But it is made infinitely more possible because of the community we are privileged to be part of. And for that, we are profoundly grateful.

About the Authors

Jai Singh Arun is a distinguished technology executive, author, and global thought leader with over 25 years of experience driving innovation in cybersecurity, quantum-safe cryptography, AI, blockchain, and emerging technologies. He leads IBM's global strategy and product management for Quantum Safe solutions. Jai has held pivotal roles across strategy, product development, marketing, and business development leadership at IBM, Unisys, Tata, and high-growth startups. He holds an MBA from UNC Chapel Hill, an M.E. in Computer Engineering from VJTI, University of Mumbai, a B.E. in Computer Science from MANIT, Bhopal, and executive education from Harvard Business School. A holder of multiple patents, Jai is also a co-author of the *Blockchain for Business* (Jai Singh Arun, Jerry Cuomo, and Nitin Gaur, May 2019, Pearson) book.

Ray Harishankar is an IBM Fellow focused on Quantum Safe. He led the overall business and technical strategy for IBM Quantum Safe, product engineering, and thought leadership. He is engaged with clients across banking, insurance, telco, and government. Ray is sought after for the pragmatic application of leading-edge technologies and innovative methods and approaches. He is on the technology advisory council for selected clients and universities. Ray was nominated as a Distinguished Engineer in 2003, an IBM Fellow in 2006, Asian American Engineer of the Year in 2009, and a Distinguished Alumni of The Ohio State University in 2013, and named in Marquis Who's Who in 2024. Ray holds 25 patents.

 **Dr. Walid Rjaibi,** Distinguished Engineer and Chief Architect for Quantum Safe at IBM, has shaped data security across multiple dimensions for over two decades. He has held pivotal roles at IBM, including CTO for Data Security, Chief Security Architect for DB2, and Research Staff Member. With a PhD in Computer Science and 28 patents, he has pioneered foundational technologies such as transparent database encryption and advanced access controls. A recognized researcher and thought leader, he bridges cutting-edge science with real-world cybersecurity. Walid is also an Adjunct Professor at Toronto Metropolitan University and advises leading cybersecurity and engineering programs across North America.

Index